W9-DJE-966

Aboriginal Reconciliation and the Dreaming

CULTURAL SURVIVAL STUDIES
IN ETHNICITY AND CHANGE

Allyn & Bacon

Series Editors, David Maybury-Lewis and Theodore Macdonald, Jr.,
Cultural Survival, Inc., Harvard University

Indigenous Peoples, Ethnic Groups, and the State,
by David Maybury-Lewis

Malaysia and the "Original People": A Case Study of the Impact of Development on Indigenous Peoples,
by Robert Knox Dentan, et al.

Gaining Ground? Evenkis, Land, and Reform in Southeastern Siberia, by Gail A. Fondahl

Ariaal Pastorialists of Kenya: Surviving Drought and Development in Africa's Arid Lands, by Elliot Fratkin

Ethnicity and Culture amidst New "Neighbors": The Runa of Ecuador's Amazon Region, by Theodore Macdonald, Jr.

Aboriginal Reconciliation and the Dreaming: Warramiri Yolngu and the Quest for Equality, by Ian S. McIntosh

Defending the Land: Sovereignty and Forest Life in James Bay Cree Society, by Ronald Niezen

Forest Dwellers, Forest Protectors: Indigenous Models for International Development, by Richard Reed

Aboriginal Reconciliation and the Dreaming:

Warramiri Yolngu and the Quest for Equality

Ian S. McIntosh
Cultural Survival, Inc.

Allyn and Bacon
Boston • London • Toronto • Sydney • Tokyo • Singapore

'Father you gave us the Dreaming'

Rev. Dr. Djiniyini Gondarra 1988

Series Editor: Sarah L. Kelbaugh
Editor-in-Chief, Social Science: Karen Hanson
Series Editorial Assistant: Jennifer DiDomenico
Marketing Manager: Brooke Stoner
Manufacturing Buyer: Julie McNeil
Cover Administrator: Jenny Hart
Editorial-Production Service: Omegatype Typography, Inc.

Copyright © 2000 by Allyn & Bacon
A Pearson Education Company
Needham Heights, Massachusetts 02494

Internet: www.abacon.com

All rights reserved. No part of the material protected by this copyright
notice may be reproduced or utilized in any form or by any means,
electronic or mechanical, including photocopying, recording, or by any
information storage and retrieval system, without the written permission
of the copyright holder.

ISBN: 0-205-29793-5

Printed in the United States of America

10 9 8 7 6 5 4 3 2 1   04 03 02 01 00 99

All photographs are credited to Ian S. McIntosh.

Contents

Foreword to the Series

Cultural Survival is an organization founded in 1972 to defend human rights of indigenous peoples, who, like the Indians of the Americas, have been dominated and marginalized by peoples different from themselves. Since the states that claim jurisdiction over indigenous peoples consider them aliens and inferiors, they are among the world's most underprivileged minorities, facing a constant threat of physical extermination and cultural annihilation. This is no small matter, for indigenous peoples make up approximately five percent of the world's population. Most of them wish to become successful ethnic minorities, meaning that they be permitted to maintain their own traditions even though they are out of the mainstream in the countries where they live. Indigenous peoples hope, therefore, for multiethnic states that will tolerate diversity in their midst. In this their cause is the cause of ethnic minorities worldwide and is one of the major issues of our times, for the vast majority of states in the world are multiethnic. The question is whether states are able to recognize and live peaceably with ethnic differences, or whether they will treat them as an endless source of conflict.

Cultural Survival works to promote multiethnic solutions to otherwise conflictive situations. It sponsors research, advocacy, and publications that examine situations of ethnic conflict, especially (but not exclusively) as they affect indigenous peoples, and suggests solutions for them. It also provides technical and legal assistance to indigenous peoples and organizations.

This series of monographs entitled "The Cultural Survival Studies in Ethnicity and Change" is published in collaboration with Allyn & Bacon, a division of Pearson Education. It will focus on problems of ethnicity in the modern world and how they affect the interrelations among indigenous peoples, ethnic groups, and the state.

The studies will focus on the situations of ethnic minorities and of the indigenous peoples, who are a special kind of ethnic minority, as they try to defend their rights, their resources, and their ways of life within modern states. Some of the volumes in the series will deal with general themes, such as ethnic conflict, indigenous rights, socioeconomic development, or multiculturalism. These volumes will contain brief case studies to illustrate their general arguments. Meanwhile, the series as a whole plans to publish a larger number of books that deal in depth with specific cases. It is our conviction that good case studies are essential for a better understanding of issues that arouse such passion in the world today, and this series will provide them. Its emphasis nevertheless will be on relating the particular to the general in the comparative contexts of national or international affairs.

The books in the series will be short, averaging approximately 160 pages in length, and written in a clear and accessible style aimed at students and the general reader. They are intended to clarify issues that are often obscure or misunderstood and that are not treated succinctly elsewhere. It is our hope, therefore, that they will also prove useful as reference works for scholars and policy makers.

David Maybury-Lewis
Theodore Macdonald, Jr.
Cultural Survival, Inc.
96 Mount Auburn St., 2nd Floor
Cambridge, Massachusetts 02138
(617) 441-5400
fax: (617) 441-5417
e-mail: csinc@cs.org
website: www.cs.org

Preface

This book represents the outcome of my studies with Australian Aborigines from the remote Northern Territory settlement of Galiwin'ku, Elcho Island, in northeast Arnhem Land. Material for this book was gathered between 1992 and 1994, while I was working towards a PhD in anthropology at the Northern Territory University. My topic was Aboriginal reconciliation. The possibility of a treaty being signed by indigenous and nonindigenous peoples by the end of the millenium was a much debated topic in Australia in the late 1990s. Yet in 1788 when the British founded the penal settlement of New South Wales there was scant official recognition of the presence or rights of Aborigines and Torres Strait Islanders. Is it too late to contemplate a pact with Australia's indigenous peoples? What form would such a treaty take and who would benefit?

In my thesis I was interested in how Elcho Islanders approached the subject of treaty negotiations, given that for perhaps 200 years prior to European occupation of Australia, these Arnhem Landers had traded with and worked for visiting Macassan fishermen from Sulawesi in Indonesia. It has been speculated, for instance, that Arnhem Landers were better able to withstand the coming of Europeans, given their prior exposure to outside ideas and influences. I began my inquiries by asking what was the relevance of the memory of these contacts for contemporary Aboriginal land and sea rights struggles. This evolved into a review of Aboriginal treaty proposals. Detailed discussions between myself and Aboriginal leaders took place both in their homes and mine, and on a number of homelands or outstations which surround the main community living area. In particular I worked with members of the Warramiri clan, one of twelve clan groups resident on Elcho Island. The Warramiri had the most detailed narratives concerning contact with Macassans and other non-Aborigines and were willing to discuss their sacred stories (traditional Aboriginal religion is referred to as the Dreaming).

I had been closely associated with this Aboriginal (Yolngu) community of Galiwin'ku for some years before undertaking these studies. As an adopted member of the Wangurri clan, and in my capacity as Homelands education supervisor, I had for many years been viewed as a mediator between Aborigines and non-Aborigines. For instance, in 1987 I was asked by Warramiri leaders to assist in the production of a prototype for a new Australian flag and to organize for the dissemination of information pertaining to it. As part of this work, I was told sacred or "inside" narratives from the Dreaming. This was not, Warramiri clan elder David Burrumarra said, so that I could parade these stories in front of a non-Aboriginal audience for my own self-interest. Rather it was so I could work for Yolngu for the furtherance of their ambitions, which in this case was the achievement of a composition or treaty between Aborigines and non-Aborigines in Australia.

All discussions referred to in this book were held in public and there was symbolic value in the way interviews were conducted. (A glossary is provided at the end to assist readers.) Burrumarra and his brothers Liwukang and Wulanybuma were already aged when I first met them, and I was considerably younger. They played up this point, that is, the elder Aborigines and the younger non-Aboriginal, the "old hands" teaching the newcomer. For them it was symbolic of Warramiri mediating traditions and, more generally, of the way relationships between Aborigines and non-Aborigines in Australia should be viewed. Aborigines are the first Australians, and while this fact is openly acknowledged by Australian government authorities, that is where recognition ends. This has to change, they said.

I wish to thank all the people of Galiwin'ku, especially the late David Burrumarra, as well as Timothy Buthimang, Joanne Garngulkpuym, George Dayngumbu, and Tracy Djoymi. Thanks also to David Mearns, my PhD supervisor, and to my dissertation examiners Howard Morphy, Ian Keen, and Robert Tonkinson, and to David and Pia Maybury-Lewis of Cultural Survival, for providing the opportunity to spread the message of Aboriginal reconciliation to an international audience. My gratitude is also extended to Ken Lum, Jeremy Beckett, Jitendra Kumarage, Paul Hayes, and Jeff Stead, who each provided criticism for particular chapters. Most especially, I wish to acknowledge the encouragement and editorial assistance of my father Stuart McIntosh, my mother Jean McIntosh, and my wife Karen...Bravo.

The Warramiri, 1920 Onwards

Stingray and catfish from the sheltered blue waters of the Arafura Sea roast on the coals. Baking in another fire are two goanna and the golden bandicoot from the rainforests behind the seashore, snared with the help of semi-tame dingoes. In baler shells are handfuls of crunchy water chestnuts, fresh black-lipped oysters, and dozens of turtle and seagull eggs. It had been a good day of hunting, thought the Warramiri clan patriarch, Ganimbirrngu. The men, mostly his sons, had gone out early in their dug-out sailing canoes, traveling up through the reef-lined channels to sites off the islands of Wirrku and Unbirri, where only male clan members can visit. Although they harpooned no turtle, with fishing lines and spears they caught plenty of fish and collected other tasty morsels, and were greeted with cheers of delight by the children as they helped pull the canoes onto the beach. The women, six of whom were the wives of Ganimbirrngu, along with their mothers, and Ganimbirrngu's female children, after collecting firewood and clearing out the waterholes of accumulating debris, had successfully scoured the wetlands for native foods.

Now as the sun set on Nangingburra, on the far northern tip of Elcho Island, the Yolngu sat around the fire and reaped the rewards of their toil. With stomachs full, they sang songs for enjoyment, and also discussed the days ahead. From this headland, Ganimbirrngu could clearly make out a collection of small fires perhaps twenty kilometers to the south. Wadangayu was the camping place of the Gupapuyngu leader Batju and his family. Both the country and the people there were called "grandparent" by the Warramiri and, through kinship, the Gupapuyngu called the Warramiri "grandchild." A sacred ceremony was soon to begin in Gupapuyngu territory and the Warramiri would all go there to stay for a month or more, joining clans from throughout the region. The Gupapuyngu liked to have lots of visitors, for their land is even more bountiful than that of the Warramiri, especially at this time of the year.

Ganimbirrngu's son Burrumarra loved to visit Wadangayu in the dry season, that half of the year when the skies were clear and the water sparkling. There was much happiness and freedom. The fish were jumping, making everyone laugh with excitement thinking about the richness of their country and time. Burrumarra believed that there was a special rock at Wadangayu that made people's lives joyous. The country and everything in it is divided into halves or moieties. This was Yirritja land belonging to Yirritja peoples like him.

At a two-day walk south of Gupapuyngu land, at the southern tip of Elcho Island, Ganimbirrngu noticed towering clouds of smoke. This was Galiwin'ku, in Dhuwa moiety country belonging to the Liyagawumirr and Gunbirrtji clans and the patriarch Banburruwuy. The Warramiri often trade with, and procure wives from, these Dhuwa moiety clans, but they know not to visit now. There has been warfare between the Dhuwa clans over suspected misuse of sacred paraphernalia, and jealousy and competition over who had rights to marry women from the mainland tribes. The strife was not yet over.

Banburruwuy was setting fire to the country, an annual occurrence, as a sign of his care and interest in its well-being. It is also an aid in hunting. Land to the Aborigines is treated as an entity with feelings. Its happiness is reliant upon the attention it gets. It needs to be worried about for it gets lonely. It longs to feel the pounding of feet when a ceremony is performed and delights in the sound of children playing, although this must be in "safe" areas, far from the sacred places. In July or August of each year, the men set the long grass ablaze and the land emits an audible "aaaahh" sound, for it recognizes the presence of law keepers.

Ceremonies are also held at this time, and because the Liyagawumirr are Dhuwa and the Warramiri Yirritja, Ganimbirrngu has no business going to Galiwin'ku. But he would encourage his sister's resident Dhuwa husbands to join in this "business," as it is called. Aboriginal society prides itself on the level of personal freedom. The only restriction is that the sacred laws of the Dreaming, the body of myths and legends which guide and animate the generation, are not breached.

•   •   •

Ganimbirrngu's children were now mostly all adults with families of their own. By the age of thirteen, his daughters, of whom there were many, had gone to live in the land of their Dhuwa moiety husbands-to-be. Only his sons remained with him. At Nangingburra, the oldest and most responsible was Djarrambi, who often made clan decisions in league with his father. Then there was Nyambi, who resented and sometimes attacked with spears the occasional Japanese fishermen because they tried to steal his wives. Mattjuwi excelled in canoe-making and had a sprinkling of pidgin English which he had picked up on the two or three trips he had made to Darwin, the only city on the coast, 500 kilometers to the west. Gawirrin was a master hunter and could easily pluck fish from the ocean's depths with his beautifully crafted three-pronged spears. Wathi, on the other hand, was sickly and suffered from leprosy, possibly introduced by the Indonesian traders who had long fished for *trepang*, or sea cucumber, on the coast in the wet season. Another son, Balwutjmi, was somewhat of a loner, and he refused to hunt, preferring to sit with the women. His existence was ignored by the male members of the clan. Then there was Liwukang, who stayed very close to the clan elders Ganimbirrngu and his "second father" Bambung and followed their every command. Burrumarra, one of the youngest, was different from the others. From the earliest age, he understood the laws of the Dreaming and had mastered a repertoire of more than one hundred Dreaming-related song cycles. He also knew love magic and sorcery, and even the sacred stories from other clans.

Ganimbirrngu believed that Burrumarra had a special gift. This young student of Aboriginal law knew that the Dhuwa moiety ancestor Djang'kawu had created the world Yirritja people lived in, but that it had been shaped by the actions of totemic beings such as the duck, octopus and whale, his clan's emblems. He was aware, also, that the social laws which govern interaction between Aborigines had been established by the Yirritja moiety founder, Lany'tjun. Though Burrumarra was still young, Ganimbirrngu decided he would break with custom and tell his child about the deeper aspects of the Warramiri Dreaming. In particular, there was the complex and often contradictory legacy of a Dreaming entity called Birrinydji. At one point in the far distant past, Warramiri Aborigines were white and enjoyed the wealth of non-Aborigines, but now they were black and poor. Knowledge is passed on just a little at a time, lest the hearer become confused and, well before his contemporaries, Burrumarra wondered to himself what must have gone wrong at the "beginning of time" for this transition to have occurred. What must happen in the future to put race relations on an equitable footing?

For hundreds of years, Macassans from Indonesia had visited these shores, but now, in the 1920s, they no longer came. Ganimbirrngu, like his father and his father's father, had grown used to having access to trade goods like tobacco, cloth, and metals. But the Macassan leader Daeng Rangka had told Ganimbirrngu that the white man no longer wanted them coming to Arnhem Land. They were being driven off at gunpoint. Yes, they had introduced diseases like small pox, and yes, there had been bloodshed at many sites over breaches of etiquette, but for many clans this trade had become a fixed and essential part of their yearly schedule. The 1920s were times of hardship, for there was no other source of the prized trade items, save by traveling to Darwin. Well to the east and west, church missions were being established, and Aborigines were leaving their country in droves to join them. The land was starting to become depopulated and that vital exchange that used to take place with mainland Aboriginal clans for stone tools and bamboo spear shafts was no more. Whites were encroaching on all sides, and while clan groups on Elcho Island still maintained their traditional ways, they were beginning to feel both isolated and besieged.

By the late 1920s Ganimbirrngu was worried. His health was in decline. Of all his family, he chose the young Burrumarra to be the one to find out about the whites, to learn from them, and to ensure that the good life he had known as a child could be available to future generations. It was right for a person of the Warramiri clan to take on such a role, Ganimbirrngu advised Burrumarra, because they were the custodians of the laws of Birrinydji—the whiteman Dreaming—white being the color associated with the wealth that rightly belonged to the Aborigines.

• • •

Not long after this decision was made Ganimbirrngu died—well before his time, other patriarchs declared at his funeral. Out of respect for the leader, members of the neighboring Gupapuyngu and Wangurri clans came to collect Burrumarra and delivered him by canoe to the newly established mission at Milingimbi about 80 kilometers to the southwest. But he didn't stay long. In the 1930s a new mission was being established at Yirrkala, closer to the major and largely deserted Warramiri homelands of Dholtji, MataMata, and Nyikala. Burrumarra was selected by missionaries as the person to make contact with these distant "warlike" clans.

Without knowing it, Burrumarra was embarking on a journey that would lead him away from his homeland forever. Never again would he awake on the sandy beach, with the dew in his face, to the sound of his kin preparing for the day's outing, and reach for whatever turtle meat was left from the night before, to heat up on the still-smouldering fire. Within a year of Burrumarra's departure, his brother Wathi died from complications linked to leprosy, and Balwutjmi was stung by a box jelly fish on the chest and drowned. A similar fate awaited Gawirrin a few years later when on a canoe trip to the sacred islands just to the north of Nangingburra. His flimsy dug-out craft was overturned in a storm and he was eaten alive by sharks. But Burrumarra would always be reminded of the fire that symbolizes the communal and energetic life of the group when at night he looked to the Southern Cross. In Aboriginal mythology, it is the fire that burns brightly in wait of the hunters who strayed too far from their land and were whisked away into the unknown by a waterspout. Soon they would be united.

When the mission came to Galiwin'ku in 1942, there was no one living at Nangingburra or at Wadangayu. They had all died or moved on to other communities. Burrumarra was a mission leader in his own right now. By the 1960s, like other Arnhem Land Aboriginal leaders, he was calling for land rights and autonomy for Aborigines nationwide. Cherished were his memories of the bush life, and the words of his mother Wanambiwuy and Ganimbirrngu's sister, Bamatja, who told him, "Don't run away from the land or hide yourself. Stand up." His younger brothers Liwukang and Wulanybuma, and his now widowed sister Rruwayi stayed close by him and his wife Lawuk, and together they held on tightly to the beliefs they had acquired as youths and applied these rigorously in all their various interactions with non-Aborigines.

•   •   •

Burrumarra had a vision of a united Australia that was drawn from long years of contemplating the Dreaming. His philosophy was as follows: Yolngu clans are affiliated with each other and with the moiety in ways which promote both a sense of unity and of diversity. Burrumarra would use the English expression *membership-and-remembership* when discussing the significance of Aboriginal law to his generation, or when promoting the building of partnerships between indigenous and nonindigenous peoples. He said that Aborigines remember or honor their specific family lineages and personal totems when Elcho Islanders unite and celebrate their membership in a clan. Similarly, Aborigines remember or uphold the laws of their clans when circumstances require that moiety issues be discussed or the journeys of Dreaming beings are ceremonially reenacted. As members of a community which includes whites, Aborigines also acknowledge that non-Aborigines occupy a significant place in the worldly scheme of things. The Birrinydji narratives, for instance, imply that whites should recognize and respect the rights of the Aborigines as keepers of the law. For Burrumarra membership-and-remembership was a policy of crucial importance in the promotion of what has become known nationally as the quest for Aboriginal reconciliation. As the first step, Burrumarra believed, whites and blacks Australia-wide must not only grasp the momentousness of the Dreaming, but respect the various levels of membership it entails and bring honor to these relationships.

2

A Divided Nation

The stunning vistas and splendid isolation of the Outback are hard to appreciate when "you can hear the Aborigines crying in the wind" (Reynolds 1998) and you know that much of the land is vacant primarily as a result of the colonizing effort. Many a citizen has been filled with enduring shame and guilt over the historical treatment of Aborigines by Australians of British descent, whether convict, squatter, or free settler. Yet vast areas of Australia are vacant not because of massacres or dispersal, but because Australian Courts promoted the British legal doctrine of *terra nullius* (or land without people) and government policy facilitated the removal of Aborigines to reserves and their children to white foster parents, in their "best interests." This legacy of Aboriginal suffering does not attract the same attention or culpability in the eyes of the wider Australian public.

Non-Aboriginal Australians are far removed in time and place from either the scenes of massacres or the major centers of Aboriginal population, yet in the 1990s white Australians exert an overwhelming influence on Aboriginal lives. They do this in a number of ways: at an ideological level, by agreeing or disagreeing that the Aborigines have rights that should be recognized by common law; at a practical level, by employing Aborigines in their businesses or illegally barring them from their establishments; and on a personal level, by their willingness or reluctance to live with and learn from Aborigines. However, the primary influence through which non-Aborigines determine the fate of Aborigines, is at the ballot box. The question of what rights Aborigines should enjoy in relation to the average citizen divide the nation.

The 1990s have witnessed an unprecedented groundswell of support for a rapprochement between the races. In 1991, a Council for Aboriginal Reconciliation was established with a vision statement that guides all its endeavors: *A united Australia which respects this land of ours; values the Aboriginal and Torres Strait Islander heritage; and provides justice and equity for all.* The response in the non-Aboriginal community to the establishment of the council has been astonishing and, some would add, long overdue.[1] In 1997, for example, the Uniting Church of Australia apologized to the Aboriginal people for their past practice of removing children from their parents and for the pain and suffering caused to those who have lost their connection with "country."[2] Also in 1997, the Catholic Church in southeast Queensland organized huge gatherings of non-Aboriginal school children in support of Aboriginal reconciliation. Pastoralists (ranchers), loggers, and Aborigines, in the spirit of rapprochement, have entered into historic (though largely symbolic) agreements with respect to land use in the Cape York Peninsula area of Queensland. The theme of the 1998 International Women's Day March in Australia was "women unite for justice and native title." Many Australian academics have also signed petitions and given their overwhelming support to continued progress in the recognition of Aboriginal rights.

Perhaps the most visible public sign of interest in Aboriginal reconciliation by non-Aborigines is the growing "Sea of Hands" sculptures found on the grounds of the Federal Parliament House in Canberra, at Bondi Beach in Sydney and in the Botanical Gardens in Brisbane. More than 100,000 multicolored hand sculptures, each carrying the name of an individual who supports (raises one's hand in favor of) reconciliation and native title, have so far been planted.

Yet despite very clear goals, reconciliation is an issue that is far from understood by the average Australian. From the Latin *concilio*, reconciliation means "to call back together again." In the minds of many, signing a hand sculpture and placing it in the "Sea of Hands" is innocuous enough. In a quote from a Brisbane paper, the *Courier-Mail*, a mother is reported to have explained to her child that the "sea of hands" meant that white and black Australians should be equal before the law. Others say it means giving Aborigines a "fair go," or that non-Aborigines are sorry for their treatment of the world's oldest living cultural group. This type of ambiguity has characterized the debate on reconciliation. A study of articles in Australian newspapers reveals that there are seven prominent positions with regard to the subject, and any one of them could be a reason for planting a hand in the name of reconciliation. Yet the inevitable outcome, if any one were to succeed, would be very different. All have varying degrees of support from both Aborigines and non-Aborigines, and I have labelled them as follows:

---

1. Aborigines received that most basic of human rights, the right to vote, only in 1967.

2. "Country" for Aborigines and Torres Strait Islanders refers to the conception and birth place and sites in the landscape associated with the creation.

Human rights reconciliation

1. justice before reconciliation
2. genocide

Economic reconciliation

3. pay your own way
4. equality before the law

Identity reconciliation

5. no indigenous viewpoint
6. building a future together as a single nation
7. membership and remembership

1. The *justice-before-reconciliation* argument encompasses a range of positions, from north Queensland Aboriginal Murandoo Yanner's "Holy crusade against murderous invaders" (*Courier-Mail* 4/18/98), where proponents have little faith in the non-Aboriginal concept of justice and therefore of reconciliation, to western Australian Aboriginal Pat Dodson's more broadly popular appeal for social justice through a restructuring of the administration of Aboriginal affairs in order to facilitate Aboriginal self-determination. The basic argument is that Aborigines have not conceded ownership of Australia, and although some groups have been successful in obtaining land title through Crown grant, other groups have not consented to the extinguishment of their native title. For reconciliation to be a reality, this injustice must be addressed.

South Africa's Truth and Reconciliation Commission and New Zealand's Treaty of Waitangi Tribunal provide models for the achievement of this form of reconciliation. A prerequisite is a thorough examination of historical truths resulting in concrete outcomes. In South Africa it is terms of imprisonment for perpetrators of hate crimes, whereas in New Zealand it is the granting of land rights to the indigenous Maori population.

2. The *genocide* argument focuses on the unfortunate living circumstances of Aborigines in both urban and rural communities. Aboriginal infant mortality rates are many times higher than in the non-Aboriginal community, and Aborigines are dying of illnesses that are readily treatable. Often compared to conditions in some African countries, the enormity of the social, physical, and health problems of Aborigines is often ignored in the heated debate about native title in Australian law courts and houses of Parliament. As Aboriginal author Rosemary O'Grady says, genocide is going on while the government and do-gooders, black and white, sit back. "It is okay to

talk of reconciliation and being sorry for the past. But until the unemployment, "grog" (alcohol), and violence problems are addressed, there will be no change" (*Courier-Mail*, 3/21/98). Discussion about a treaty should be temporarily set aside and attention focused on ameliorating the pressing problems of Aboriginal survival into the twenty-first century.

3. The *pay-your-own-way* argument is closely related to the above, suggesting that the $16 billion expended on Aboriginal welfare over the past 13 years has done nothing but line the pockets of bureaucrats and other non-Aborigines. No appreciable improvement is detectable in the deplorable housing, health, education, or employment conditions of the nation's indigenous people. The federal government policy of self-determination for Aborigines, according to this argument, has facilitated exploitative activities by non-Aboriginal entrepreneurs, made possible by Aboriginal mismanagement of taxpayers' funds. While Aborigines believe themselves to be victims of institutional racism, non-Aborigines respond with a claim of institutional irresponsibility on the part of indigenous organizations. "Justice must not only be seen to be done for Aborigines by the other 98 percent of Australians, who largely bear the cost of Aboriginal justice and welfare. They must be able to see that their tax-dollar contributions are not being wasted" (*Courier-Mail* 4/18/98). It is acknowledged that Aborigines require financial assistance, but indigenous people should be encouraged to contribute toward paying their way.

This argument also highlights the circumstances in which sacred traditions are perceived to be invented by Aborigines seeking justice in order to block projects vital to the nation's economic development. It is suggested that many Aborigines are angry at the way their culture and history are being manipulated and distorted for short-term political and economic ends. The Hindmarsh Island bridge fiasco is a case in point. Here, Aborigines were accused of making fraudulent claims about the sanctity of a site to forestall a development, and one group of Aboriginal women stood up to defend the integrity of their past and denounce the Aboriginal activists. One of the leaders of that group, South Australian Aboriginal Beryl Kropinyeri, is viewed by some as a stalwart for the sort of reconciliation that is achievable and desirable for Australia. Criticizing both black and white Australians for manipulating the past in order to meet some short-term agenda, she asserts, "Reconciliation starts with the truth."

4. The *equality-before-the-law* argument is analagous to the one used by opponents of affirmative action in the United States, that is, indigenous people have no more and no less right to basic community services than anyone else. How can there be one law for non-Aborigines

and another for Aborigines in the same nation? Why should Aborigines have a right to negotiate for developments on their land when non-Aborigines do not enjoy such a right? Alternatively there is a desire to "wipe clean the slate" and have all land claims finalized here and now, either through grants of land or financial compensation, as was proposed in the United States in the 1940s with the Indian Claims Commission. It is argued that reconciliation is a "two-way street," and it is in everyone's best interests if the playing field is leveled.

5. The *no-indigenous-viewpoint* argument is critical of the notion that an Aboriginal community exists with whom negotiations could be carried out, if a treaty were considered a desirable outcome of the reconciliation process. This argument condemns the tendency to treat contemporary black/white relations as if it were 1788 once again, with Aboriginal and non-Aboriginal Australians as two entirely separate entities. The reality is that Aboriginal and non-Aboriginal lives are completely intertwined. Aboriginality is a matter of history, upbringing, and descent, and there is tremendous diversity in contemporary Australian Aboriginal life. While proponents of reconciliation tend to stress that all Aborigines have a special spiritual connection to the land, this is not so. There is no common indigenous point of view.

6. The *building-a-future-together-as-a-single-nation* argument is the theme of the Aboriginal Reconciliation movement, and it has many adherents. Like U.S. President Bill Clinton's Initiative on Race, the ambition is to establish a dialogue on issues that divide the nation. Up until recent times, Americans, like Australians, have either refused to accept that there is a problem or simply ignored the race question. The "great Australian silence" on all matters to do with Aborigines was described by leading anthropologist Bill Stanner as a "cult of forgetfulness" or "disremembering" on a national scale. In the 1960s he called upon all Australians to consider the unacknowledged history of relations between the two racial groups.

In Australia, this discourse has a psychological dimension that has barely been broached in the debate. According to Lattas (1997), conservative political discourse celebrates Australia's pioneers and explorers. Their suffering has become the basis of white society's right of ownership of the land and, also, the means by which they are reconciled with Aborigines (1997:235). Another strand of this argument suggests that white settler Australians are alienated from, and need to be reconciled with, the harsh Australian environment, and they can do this only through Aborigines. "Reconciliation with the spirituality of Aboriginal people is posited as the means for healing that sense of...alienation [which results from] belonging to settler society"

(Lattas 1997:241). Lattas argues that a redemptive function is being assigned to Aborigines, and the process of knowing something about Aboriginal culture is taking on the form of a pilgrimage. Aborigines are posited as supremely spiritual beings and, like Native Americans in the United States, in touch with the earth and an earlier, simpler, more meaningful time. Reconciliation, from this perspective, amounts to a further colonization of the Aborigines, but this time through their religion, the Dreaming.[3] The controversy created by American author Marlo Morgan (1994) in her fictitious book about unnamed Aborigines, entitled *Mutant Message Down Under*, encapsulates this phenomenon.

7. The *membership-and-remembership* argument could be considered a response to the "great Australian silence" or "disremembering" on race relations. Simply put, it revolves around the concept of adoption: Aborigines adopting non-Aborigines into their domain and vice versa, affirming the self-worth of both parties. Non-Aborigines are landowners as a result of Aboriginal dispossession and must remember the rights of the traditional landholders. Also, Aborigines are Australian citizens, but they remember (or assert their rights as members of) a landowning language group, clan, and family. The ideology is summarized by Warramiri Aboriginal leader David Burrumarra when he says that for Aborigines human rights entail following Aboriginal law, building up one's own clan and homeland, and bringing honor to yourself, other Aborigines, and the wider Australian community.

Former high-ranking official in the Australian public service and renowned social commentator Dr. "Nugget" Coombs (1994) argued that it is only when non-Aboriginal Australian society is aware of the Aboriginal agenda for reconciliation, as detailed for instance, in the justice-before-reconciliation and membership-and-remembership viewpoints, that reconciliation can become a meaningful and achievable objective. It is my object in this book, beginning in Chapter 4, to describe comprehensively the Aboriginal agenda for reconciliation from the perspective of one group of Aborigines living in the remote Northern Territory settlement of Galiwin'ku, Elcho Island, in north-east Arnhem Land. First, however, it is necessary to set the scene for Aboriginal reconciliation. It is two hundred and ten years since the first permanent non-Aboriginal presence in Australia. Why is a treaty now considered a desirable option? How much support does the treaty have in the broader Australian community?

---

3. The Dreaming is an expression for traditional Aboriginal religion and is not applicable to the Torres Strait, though Islanders may refer to their beliefs as such.

AUSTRALIA AT THE CROSSROADS

Australia is at the crossroads. The year 2001 marks the centennial of the nation's federation and there is much soul-searching about the future of the island continent. A significant number of Australians hope that the year 2001 will herald the election of an Australian head of state in place of the nation's titular English monarch. But whether or not Australia becomes a republic, the need to achieve a lasting reconciliation with Australia's indigenous people ranks fairly high on the national agenda.

The 1990s witnessed tremendous progress in this arena. The Council for Aboriginal Reconciliation examined the feasibility of enacting a treaty or compact in time for the coming centennial. The overall aim was for the twenty-first century to usher in a new approach to black-white relations and for the new millennium to mark an end to the suffering endemic to so many Aboriginal lives since the raising of the Union Jack at Sydney Cove in January 1788.

Through repeated court challenges in the 1990s, indigenous people have made significant headway in achieving the recognition of rights to their land. In 1992, Torres Strait Islander native title was affirmed by the highest court in the land. The decision ensured similar property rights for all Australia's indigenous populations. The Native Title Act (1993), enacted in response to that great victory, put in place largely administrative procedures to deal with such recognition. This legislation acknowledges the status of indigenous people as the prior owners of the country, and also that many Aborigines were dispossessed of their land without compensation. The landmark High Court decisions of 1992 (also known as Mabo[4]) and 1996 (Wik[5]) have given some native title-holders, for the very first time, the opportunity to "sit at the table" and negotiate for employment, training, and other benefits accruing from development on lands for which they have a traditional attachment. Aboriginal and Torres Strait Islander leaders proclaim this to be the very essence of reconciliation.

Australia's constitution permits a democratically elected parliament to enact laws discriminating between peoples on the basis of race. A relic of the 1890s and the infamous White Australia Policy, this race power was used in 1967, following a national referendum, to allow the federal government to make laws for the advancement of Aborigines. In 1998 Parliament used this law to the detriment of the first Australians. The Australian government modified the Native Title Act in order to favor the interests of developers over and above

---

4. After Eddie Mabo, the Torres Strait Islander who led the court challenge.
5. For the Wik Aborigines of Cape York Peninsula

the interests of Aborigines and Islanders. The "ten point" amendment plan ruled out the possibility of native title existing on waterways and insisted that claimants have a continuing physical connection with the land being claimed, even though a majority of Aboriginal people were forcibly removed or driven off their homelands as a result of colonization. The most alarming amendment severely restricted the power of Aborigines to negotiate. This power had been described by some commentators as the single greatest breakthrough in Australian race relations in this century.

While the land-rights movement has the support of major churches and many influential non-Aborigines in southern states, indigenous people comprise only 2 percent of the nation's population and have little voting power. The Sydney 2000 Olympic Games is a prime venue for a major international protest, as Aborigines mobilize political support in this the United Nation's Decade of the World's Indigenous Peoples.

THE BEGINNING AND THE END OF THE RECONCILIATION PROCESS?

Treaty negotiations in Australia are of recent origin. In the 1970s a Treaty Committee was established by the federal government. Comprised in its entirety of non-Aborigines, the committee's function was to sell to the non-Aboriginal population the idea that a treaty or makarrata was necessary for Australia's future. On the one hand, there was a fear that if progress was not made toward the recognition of the rights and interests of Aborigines, an economic or political backlash might jeopardize the country's international standing. On the other hand, there was a genuine belief that only with the enactment of a treaty could Australians look openly and honestly at the past and build a future as a multicultural nation. As Gough Whitlam, Australia's prime minister from 1972 to 1975, proclaimed, "We are all diminished while the Aboriginal people are denied their basic rights."

Treaty consultation among Aborigines was the task of a newly established committee, the National Aboriginal Consultative Committee (NACC). However, after a number of years, it became obvious that this body was inadequate in representing the vast range of indigenous voices across Australia. There are Aborigines who have title to their own tribal lands; there are those who live on reserves or "excisions" on the world's largest cattle stations; or in "humpies," lean-to dwellings, on the outskirts of small rural towns; and there are urban dwellers who, apart from their poverty, are living a life almost indistinguishable from that of most non-Aboriginal Australians. Then there are the people of the Torres Strait, living on the islands between Australia and

Papua New Guinea. Saibai Island, for instance, lies just off the south coast of New Guinea and the principal affiliation of the inhabitants is with Fly River people and the residents of Daru in New Guinea. Similarly remote are the Aborigines of the western desert, who have little or no communication with anyone outside of their communities. Finally, there is the anomalous position of the Kanakas, primarily from the Solomon Islands, brought to east-coast sugar plantations in the 1800s as indentured laborers, some of whom now live within the Aboriginal and Islander community along the Queensland coast.

Like so many public policies and programs of the day, there was little consultation with Aborigines prior to the establishment of the NACC. Here was an institution designed by non-Aborigines, structured on principles foreign to most Aborigines, which could not possibly facilitate indigenous involvement in the reconciliation process. Apart from this, there was little support for, or interest in, a treaty on the part of Aborigines or Torres Strait Islanders. The idea put forward by the federal government as an answer to all social and economic problems was seen by Aborigines as an irrelevant pipe dream. A majority of Aborigines and Islanders wanted land and financial compensation for prior dispossession. In 1984 the Treaty Committee was disbanded.

Since that time, national parliamentary inquiries into the alarming rate of Aboriginal deaths while in police custody; into the fate of those "stolen generation" children forcibly removed from the custody of their parents "for their own good"; and into the protracted court battles between developers and Aborigines over the planned destruction of sacred sites, all point to the one conclusion. It is not possible to separate the concepts of Aboriginal and Islander identity, land and sea rights, and the reconciliation process. In 1988 at the Northern Territory Barunga Festival celebrating the survival of Aboriginal culture for 40,000 years, the then–Prime Minister Bob Hawke made a historic commitment to the negotiation and conclusion of a treaty or compact between the Commonwealth of Australia and the Aboriginal people. He invited Aborigines and Islanders to consider what the terms of such a compact would be. The outcome was the 1991 establishment of the Council for Aboriginal Reconciliation through a unanimous vote in both houses of the federal government.

The council is comprised of twenty-five members, twelve of whom are Aboriginal (one from Galiwin'ku), two are Torres Strait Islanders, and eleven are drawn from the wider Australian community. There are television personalities, business and church leaders, farmers federation representatives, and other well-known Australians. To date the task of the council has been raising the awareness and support for the reconciliation process across Australia. Reconciliation, according to the council, is a process which strives to improve relations between Aborigines and the wider community and is based on recognition of

- the unique position of indigenous people as the original inhabitants of this continent;
- the need to overcome the continuing disadvantage suffered by Aborigines and Islanders which is a legacy of policies and practices that dispossessed them from their traditional lands, separated indigenous children from their families, and actively discouraged their participation in Australia's economic and social development; and
- the creation of a confident and harmonious nation as we approach the centennial of federation in the year 2001.

The council has identified eight issues that are essential to the reconciliation process. These are the following:

1. a greater understanding of the importance of the land and sea in indigenous societies
2. better relationships between indigenous people and the wider community
3. recognition of indigenous cultures and heritage as a valued part of the Australian heritage
4. recognition by all Australians of a shared ownership of their history
5. awareness of the causes of disadvantage which prevent indigenous people from achieving fair and proper standards in health, housing, employment, and education
6. a greater community response to addressing the underlying causes of the unacceptably high levels of imprisonment for indigenous people
7. greater opportunity for indigenous people to control their destinies
8. agreement on whether the process of reconciliation would be advanced by a document of reconciliation or treaty

The work of the Reconciliation Council was divided into stages: extensive education campaigns within both the Aboriginal and non-Aboriginal communities; an examination of strategies; and the setting of a timetable for reconciliation. The struggle for Aboriginal and Torres Strait Islander land rights and reconciliation has been long and hard. As I detail in the next section, victories in the early 1990s gave way to serious setbacks in the late 1990s. With the 1998 amendments to the Native Title Act, there is little likelihood of the creation of a harmonious and confident nation by the year 2001.

LEGAL RECOGNITION OF
ABORIGINAL HUMAN RIGHTS
Legal Status

European nations had been concluding treaties with non-Christian societies for hundreds of years prior to the arrival of the English in Australia. Most were concerned with the development of commerce, though many resulted in the ceding of sovereignty in return for protection. Even in cases where the people knew nothing of what they were signing, European powers showed no hesitation because treaties were regarded as binding in international law (Sorrenson 1991: 19). But in Australia there was to be no treaty. Explorer Captain Cook was to get the consent of native inhabitants before claiming possession of the "great southern land," but when he reached Botany Bay in 1770, he simply took possession by right of discovery. Several years later, when the British Committee on Transportation was investigating possible locations for a new convict settlement, they rejected Gambia and Madagascar because it would have been necessary to purchase the required land. Instead they chose Australia, for the land in question was "waste and substantially unoccupied" and without legitimate owners with right or power to govern.[6]

In 1788 sovereignty over Australia was claimed in the name of the British Crown and the land was declared to be *terra nullius*. This discredited legal doctrine asserted that the Australian tribes had not yet arrived at a state of social improvement in which proprietary right to the soil existed.[7]

Instructions in Letters Patent to Arthur Phillip, the first governor of the new colony in 1788, was for Aborigines to have full and free right of passage on Crown land, to hunt and fish and construct their dwellings "in such a manner as they would have been entitled to if this demise had not been made." However, all over Australia, colonial governments were unable or unwilling to control or prevent the seizure of land by settlers and soldiers. Despite campaigns by Christian philanthropists, antislavery fraternities, and the Aboriginal Protection Society, indigenous inhabitants received no compensation for their losses. Attempts to defend their land through guerrilla-type warfare were fruitless. From a population of around 300,000, divided

---

6. The decision of the Committee on Transportation was influenced by gentleman scholar Sir Joseph Banks who had traveled with Cook to Australia.

7. Bermuda was *terra nullius*, but in this case there were no indigenous inhabitants.

into perhaps 300 linguistic groupings in 1788, by 1900 over 75 percent of the indigenous inhabitants were thought to have perished. Aborigines were not counted in the population census. They were invisible and soon to die out and be replaced with a fitter population. Disease and starvation had taken their toll and token protection of the survivors became official government policy in the early years of the twentieth century. Aborigines were herded onto large reservations, for instance in the state of Queensland, or occupied small camps on the outskirts of towns in New South Wales. In the far north of the country many Aborigines worked as unpaid laborers on cattle stations, which permitted them to remain on their ancestral lands and support their families in a manner somewhat reminiscent of the traditional life. This state of affairs persisted until the introduction of award wages in the 1960s, at which time many Aborigines were evicted from properties and forced en masse to the outskirts of larger townships to live in abject poverty.

After one hundred and fifty years of decline, the Aboriginal population has begun to stabilize and grow once again. In a 1967 constitutional referendum, 92 percent of Australians voted in favor of giving the Commonwealth of Australia the power to make laws on behalf of Aboriginal people and as a nation. Aborigines thus gained the first of their basic rights as Australian citizens—the right to cast a vote. Soon afterwards Aborigines began to enjoy other rights, such as greater access to medical care and schooling as well as unemployment, old age, and supporting parent pensions. The election of the Whitlam Labor government in 1972 saw for the first time substantial amounts of federal money being allocated to Aboriginal welfare and community development. An agenda of change was unfolding, and moves were afoot to create the circumstances in which Aborigines could achieve autonomy as citizens of Australia as owners of their own lands.

Land Ownership

Australia received English law in 1828 and *terra nullius* as well: the principle of the sovereign or Crown as the proprietor of all land became the basis of the Australian property system. As no land was ever granted to Aborigines, they were never vested with any form of legal title. Aborigines and Islanders were completely dispossessed, a fate shared by few other people colonized by Great Britain. Before 1992, the accepted Australian law was that any preexisting rights Aborigines enjoyed did not survive British occupation. As I detail later, the first court battle over land rights (Supreme Court 1971) was fought in the early 1970s by the Yolngu (Aborigines) of northeast Arnhem Land. In what became known as the Gove land-rights case, the decision was that Australian law did not recognize Aboriginal native title.

The first breakthrough in the recognition of Aboriginal land rights came in 1976 with the passage of the Aboriginal Land Rights (Northern Territory) Act. Under the act, Aboriginal reserves such as Arnhem Land were transferred to Aboriginal land trusts, and through a claims process, Aborigines could take up statutory title to land that they traditionally owned. This legislation was to be a model for land-rights legislation throughout Australia, but opposition by miners and cattle station owners (pastoralists) in the six states was enormously influential, and the federal government capitulated. As a result, no other Australian jurisdictions passed such laws. Only in the Northern Territory, where the Commonwealth had legislative power as a result of the 1967 referendum, did some Aborigines come to enjoy that degree of security and self-determination that the act offers.

In the 1980s, Torres Strait Islander Eddie Mabo challenged the Crown's ownership of his homeland on Murray Island (Meriam) in the far east of the straits between Queensland and Papua New Guinea, at the northern extremity of Australia's Great Barrier Reef. The decision of the High Court case overturned the Gove decision and was applicable to all Australian states: The judgment forever banished the term *terra nullius* as a valid basis of land ownership in Australia. There *is* a place in Australian common law for Aboriginal and Torres Strait Islander customary law.

The Mabo High Court judgment of 1992 has had dramatic consequences in Australia, perhaps more dramatic than would have occurred in other countries that emerged from British colonial rule. Canada and New Zealand had enacted treaties to recognize the rights of indigenous people. In the United States, courts acknowledged not only the territorial rights of Native Americans, but their political rights as sovereign entities—domestic dependent nations—within the overall sovereignty of the nation (Bravo 1997).

Eddie Mabo's challenge has transformed the nation. The court affirmed that native title has existed from time immemorial and has survived British occupation. It can, however, be extinguished by the Crown through a valid grant of title, for example, when a person purchases a property as freehold, but only if such a grant does not conflict with other Commonwealth legislation, such as the Racial Discrimination Act 1975. The Native Title Act 1993, enacted as a result of the Mabo High Court decision, regulates title found to exist in common law and has established procedures for making and adjudicating land and sea claims. It also provides for compensation where native title has been extinguished. Since its enactment, the number of native title claims has been steadily increasing, and today over 700 claims await deliberation by the National Native Title Tribunal and/or the federal court. To date, only a handful of the cases have been decided, with most favoring the Aborigines.

The enactment of native title legislation fueled a backlash against Aboriginal property rights across Australia, particularly because of the number of ambit claims being made, for instance when Aborigines lay claim to Sydney's Opera House or Brisbane's central business district. There is widespread fear of a land grab and headlines in newspapers proclaim the imminent loss of suburban backyards and gardens and detail how Aborigines and islanders will use their newfound powers to obstruct development. In places such as the Goldfields in western Australia, the mining industry suggests that many of the 42 native title claims already lodged are overlapping and that development will soon come to a standstill. Companies are adamant that the Act is unworkable. Their concern is based on the fact that some deals struck between them and particular Aboriginal groups have been made null and void by allegations from other Aborigines that the land in question actually belonged to them. Chaos reigns in the Goldfields of western Australia, and the resulting interclan and interfamily rivalry plays into the hands of developers and opponents of the new law.[8]

The actual trigger for the 1998 enactment of reactionary amendments to the Native Title Act was another historic High Court decision, this time involving the Wik Aborigines of far north Queensland. Responding to questions left unresolved by the Mabo case, the High Court in 1996 determined that the granting of pastoral leases by the Crown did not necessarily extinguish native title. Pastoral leases were a uniquely Australian response to the illegal occupation of Crown land by squatters. Designed to provide some security of tenure so that the occupiers could run their cattle, the leases were never intended to provide holders with exclusive title. The judgement in Wik was that native title may coexist with pastoral interests, though if there were a conflict between the two, pastoral interests would predominate.

The outcome of the Mabo High Court case was that perhaps only 5 percent of Australia's indigenous people would have the power to negotiate over their land. With the Wik decision, 70 percent of Australia is open to native title claims. Resistance by non-Aborigines to the possibility of having to deal with indigenous people has sent the country into turmoil. Developers and station owners who are resisting negotiation with Aborigines are concerned about their economic future and the future of the nation. The conservative government perceived two stark choices: to press ahead with amendments to the Native Title Act and endanger the reconciliation process or, alternatively, to water down the proposed amendments, keeping the

---

8. Vital and overdue anthropological research into Aboriginal land tenure needs to be completed and this process cannot be rushed.

process alive but alienating miners, pastoralists, and their even more cautious rural parliamentarians. Obviously government could not concede this, and they chose the former. All that has been gained in the past ten years appears on the verge of forfeiture.

MABO AND RECONCILIATION

One of the foremost writers on the subject of treaty negotiations, Dr. "Nugget" Coombs (1994:158), said that since the 1967 referendum, there have been at least three separate agendas determining the pattern of black–white relationships. The first is the agenda of the multinational corporate sector, led by resource-hungry enterprises, largely antagonistic to Aboriginal aspirations. Then there is the agenda of the government and its bureaucracies and its attempt to establish power bases in Aboriginal affairs and facilitate the multinational corporate agenda while maintaining the appearance of neutrality. Lastly there is the Aboriginal agenda.

Coombs was cognizant of the shortcomings of legislation as a means of building bridges between peoples. The High Court judgment that led to the proclamation of the Native Title Act did not deal with, for instance, social, political, human, or other rights. Nor did it tackle the more general legal questions of whether a fiduciary obligation of care and protection for indigenous Australians had been established with the acquisition of sovereignty by the Crown, or what were the limits to sovereignty as it then existed. Coombs argued that the enactment of native title legislation in Australia could not take the place of a treaty. In a book entitled *Aboriginal Autonomy: Issues and Strategies* (1994), Coombs stated that the federal government must go far beyond such laws or face international rebuke. He said the Native Title Act was nothing more than an attempt to validate past dispossession of land from Aborigines and to allow further forced dispossession to occur. Before his death in 1997, Coombs called for a moratorium on all legislation affecting Aborigines until such time when a "deeper act of recognition" in dealing with questions of Aboriginal self-government would be negotiated among all Aborigines across Australia. Such an act, he said, would seek "the resolution of the conflict created by white occupation in 1788 and the continuing dispossession and destruction of Aborigines and their society."

SEEKING A "COMPACT" OR "COMPOSITION"

Australian anthropologist Bill Stanner argued that Australia's Aborigines have had a conscious agenda directed at a "composition" or rapprochement with non-Aborigines ever since they realized the presence of outsiders was permanent. In places remote from the colonizing effort, Aborigines had the opportunity to adjust their lifestyles and cosmology to the changes going on all around them. The term "silent revolution" was coined by anthropologist Erich Kolig (1981) to describe the way that Aborigines were transforming their lives and tackling the problems of the new world on terms of their own choosing while remaining faithful to the Dreaming. The desired end of this revolution is not dissimilar to that being advocated by the Aboriginal Reconciliation Council—an equitable future for all. In northeast Arnhem Land, this process has been underway since precolonial times when Macassan fisherfolk from eastern Indonesia made their seasonal visits to those shores. But what Aborigines wish to achieve and what non-Aborigines are willing to concede is at variance.

3

Seeking Reconciliation

In this chapter, I summarize major points of view as presented at the Australian Reconciliation Convention in order to answer the questions: Are Aborigines and non-Aborigines arguing for reconciliation from entirely different premises? Is there a possibility of common ground? The Council for Aboriginal Reconciliation Act, 1991, requires the promotion, through leadership, education, and discussion, of a deeper understanding by all Australians of the history, cultures, past dispossession, and continuing disadvantage of indigenous Australians and of the need to redress that disadvantage. The act presents Australians with an opportunity to share responsibility for achieving progress. Indeed, the Council for Aboriginal Reconciliation measures its success by the degree to which the average Australian participates in the reconciliatory process, whether in the classroom, faith group, office, or sports field.

To date the highlight of the council's work was the staging in May 1997 of the Australian Reconciliation Convention. Bringing together community leaders from all around Australia and from all walks of life put reconciliation squarely at the center of the national political agenda. Three major areas were highlighted as being fundamental to the reconciliation process.[9] They are

- Aboriginal self-determination
- land and sea rights as basic human rights
- economic independence and the power of veto over resource exploitation

Participants at the convention downplayed areas of conflict, but close scrutiny of the many presentations made clear that there is widespread difference of opinion as to how reconciliation is or should be

---

9. In ensuing chapters, I examine each of these from the perspective of Aborigines living in the remote northern Australian community of Galiwin'ku.

defined. The one area in which there was total agreement was that if reconciliation is to succeed it must be a people's movement.

WHAT IS RECONCILIATION?

Council memoranda clearly state that reconciliation is a process which strives to improve relations between Aboriginal and Torres Strait Islander peoples and the wider community. It cannot be achieved by the council alone, nor by the nation's leaders or by acts of Parliament. Reconciliation depends on the ideas, effort, and goodwill of the community. Australian Reconciliation Convention proceedings and the many projects underway in Australia at present emphasize that the process is for all age groups and all sectors of society and is based on

- communication, trust, listening and understanding, and having a common vision
- the belief that apologies should be offered and forgiveness sought so that a process of healing may begin
- the recognition that indigenous people are equal partners at any negotiating table

In a 1997 report, then–Reconciliation Council Chairperson Pat Dodson emphasized that if reconciliation was to be more than just a utopian dream, it had to become a living reality in communities, institutions, and organizations, and "in all expressions of our common citizenship."[10] Dodson pointed to the many native title regional agreements that have already been signed around the country as evidence of the possibilities that arise when goodwill, mutual respect, and a shared objective replace the ignorance, fear, and mistrust that unfortunately so often determine Aboriginal–non-Aboriginal relationships. Dodson also made reference to some of the many examples of indigenous and other Australians working together to make reconciliation a practical reality. The National Assembly of Local Government adopted a national statement on community tolerance calling on local councils to endorse and actively promote reconciliation. International mining companies such as CRA and Western Mining have issued policy statements incorporating respect for indigenous peoples' perspectives. The National Football League has a new code of conduct which strongly condemns racism in the sport. Community members in Kempsey in New South Wales have celebrated the work of internationally acclaimed Aboriginal artists, a

---

10. From the "Call to the Nation" adopted by participants at the convention.

milestone for a community with a history of tension between non-Aborigines and Aboriginal fringe dwellers.

Other examples abound. Awards recognizing the efforts and achievements of Australians working together were presented for the first time in 1997 to schools, large corporations, private and government businesses, government agencies, churches, professional organizations, community groups, and individuals, demonstrating the extent to which practical reconciliation initiatives are being implemented throughout all sectors of Australian society.

At the final session of the Australian Reconciliation Convention in Melbourne in May 1997, over 1800 participants adopted by acclamation the "Call to the Nation," which stated:

> [R]econciliation between Australia's indigenous peoples and other Australians is central to the renewal of this nation as a harmonious and just society which lives out its national ethos of a fair go for all.... We call on our fellow Australians…to build a people's movement for reconciliation of sufficient breadth and power to guarantee that Australia can truly celebrate the centenary of its nationhood in 2001 confident that it has established a sound foundation for reconciliation.

CONVENTION DEBATES

The subject matter of contributions by the many speakers at the convention can be divided into the following categories: definitions, prerequisites, obstacles and challenges, methods and goals. Three perspectives predominate:

(a) one which downplays the importance of race and culture and focuses on alleviating economic hardship, the *economic reconciliation* (incorporating the pay-your-own-way and equality-before-the-law arguments mentioned in Chapter 2);

(b) one which emphasizes race and culture, native title, and self-determination, the *human rights reconciliation* (incorporating the justice-before-reconciliation and genocide arguments); and

(c) one which attempts to delineate the common ground, dealing with the more fundamental issue of national identity, the *identity reconciliation* (incorporating the membership-and-remembership, no-indigenous-viewpoint, and building-a-future-together-as-a-single-nation arguments).

Immediately clear from reading the various contributions of government, religious, industry, and indigenous leaders is that participants argue for reconciliation on different premises. One side stresses the practical aspects, another the theoretical, and the third the spiritual or metaphysical. Aboriginal Council member Linda Burnley, for instance, believes that reconciliation is a self-help project, whereas international guest speaker Mililani Trask of Hawaii argues that a national apology is a necessary first stage in the reconciliation process. Anglican Archbishop Peter Carnley, on the other hand, emphasizes the need to attend to the deep spiritual bonds that characterize a more wholesome relationality among persons of different race and culture in a socially unified community.

In her introduction to a session convened to discuss the meaning of the term reconciliation, Professor of Aboriginal Studies at the Northern Territory University and Aboriginal Reconciliation Council member, Marcia Langton, outlined the options facing the nation. She said, "We have the choice of cooperating for the larger good through reconciliation or continuing the conflict, which undermines our national potential for well-being and success." She discussed potential obstacles. One is a general perception prevalent in the non-Aboriginal community that only Aborigines want reconciliation: It will bring advantages to Aborigines that other Australians do not enjoy. Alternatively, non-Aborigines assert, "Yes, it would be a good thing if Aborigines reconciled with Australia, then they might be more useful to society." Aborigines and Islanders respond by saying, "Look at what they've done to us. They don't understand us. They are under constant pressure to misunderstand us. Why should we reconcile?" Professor Langton noted that the challenge is to clarify what reconciliation means, and she stressed that it is a subject of national importance.

The Australian Reconciliation Convention provided Aborigines with an opportunity to offer their views on the subject of reconciliation. Of the speakers present were three from the northeast Arnhem Land Aboriginal community of Yirrkala (Mandawuy Yunupingu, Galarrwuy Yunupingu, and Yalmay Yunupingu), and one from Galiwin'ku (Rev. Dr. Djiniyini Gondarra). A sampling of delegates comments, gathered below, illuminate the characteristics of, and contrasts between, different perspectives. They range from straightforward and forceful to wooly and well-meaning vacuity. In summary, Aboriginal contributions to the reconciliation debate tend to be short and to the point. Demands are clearcut. Yet so many of the comments of non-Aboriginal conference participants cannot lead to action. They are well-meaning to the point of banality. While there is such division as to what reconciliation means, progress can only be expected to be limited.

Definitions

Economic reconciliation

- Reconciliation means taking the initiative towards ensuring an accessible and continually developing process of consultation with Aborigines—one that will become fundamental to the way we do business. (The Right Hon. Lord Mayor Cr I. Deveson AO, City of Melbourne)

Human rights reconciliation

- Reconciliation means being able to exercise our right to our traditional lands and resources. We want to have our say in how resources are developed and to share in the benefits of such development. (Tracker Tilmouth, Director, Central Land Council)

Identity reconciliation

- Reconciliation is a religious and moral term; it addresses such realities as anger, alienation, abuse, pain and hurt, prejudice. (The Most Rev. Dr. Peter Carnley, Anglican Archbishop of Perth)

Goals

Economic reconciliation

- We as a nation are at the most important point in our history. What sort of society do we want? Reconciliation is a key issue if equitable outcomes are to be a reality for all Australians. (Dr. R. Alwis, Chair of the Federation of Ethnic Communities' Councils of Australia)

Human rights reconciliation

- A document of reconciliation should be negotiated between all indigenous and nonindigenous Australians and put into legislation by the federal parliament. It is critical that there is a sense of ownership of it (Noel Pearson, Legal Advisor, ATSIC)

Identity reconciliation

- What is it that we would like to be known for? Our cotton farming? Our gold mining? Or for our sense of tolerance and our commitment to diversity? (Mr. H. Glenn, Director, National Australia Day Council)

Prerequisites

Economic reconciliation

- To sustain life in our pastoral areas, Aboriginal communities require profitable operations and adequate government services and infrastructure such as telecommunications, transport, health, and education services. (Mr. P. Day, South Australian Farmers Federation, South Australia)

Human rights reconciliation

- If native title is taken away, then everything is lost and Australia has lost its chance for reconciliation. (Galarrwuy Yunupingu AM, Chair, Northern Land Council, Darwin)

Identity reconciliation

- Aboriginal culture must be recognized and accepted as an intrinsic element of our national identity. (Mandawuy Yunupingu AM, Lead Singer, Yothu Yindi)

Obstacles/Challenges

Economic reconciliation

- Indigenous people are locked into a cycle of poverty and are heavily reliant on welfare. The dispossession of indigenous people from their lands has denied them opportunities for economic participation. (Joseph Elu, Aboriginal and Torres Strait Islander Commercial Development Corporation)

Human rights reconciliation

- Reconciliation must come from the heart not the head. We are waiting for actions that will make us believe that the true spirit of reconciliation has finally arrived in Australia. (Wayne Connolly, Chairman, Aboriginal Coordinating Council, Queensland)

Identity reconciliation

- There is a gnawing sense of a divisive "them" and "us" mentality which political parties like Pauline Hanson's "One Nation" are happy to exploit. (Dr. R. Alwis, Chair of the Federation of Ethnic Communities' Councils of Australia)

Methods

Economic reconciliation

- Industry has to understand and acknowledge indigenous objectives and how these can interact with opportunities for economic independence through participation in industry. (Mr. J. Ellis, President, Minerals Council of Australia)

Human rights reconciliation

- Hearing the stories of Aborigines face to face transforms statistics from empty figures into a human reality. (Her Excellency Lady Helen Deane)

Identity reconciliation

- There must be a recognition of customary law in such a way that the two systems can be gradually harmonized and tailored to meet the needs of particular communities. (Mr. G. Nicholson, Senior Crown Counsel for the Northern Territory)

SELF-DETERMINATION AND RECONCILIATION

In a publication produced by the Council for Aboriginal Reconciliation entitled "The Path to Reconciliation, Issues for a People's Movement," self-determination is defined as fundamental to the process of reconciliation:

> Self-determination is a universal human right of all peoples. It can be defined as the right of distinct groups of people, with a shared culture and history, to pursue their lifestyles and culture in a manner consistent with their own traditions…. For Aboriginal and Torres Strait Islander peoples, self-determination means having a say about how to live now and in the future. This includes such rights as maintaining and teaching cultures and languages…and managing natural resources on the land. The challenge for all Australians is to work out ways to enable indigenous Australians to exercise their rights to self-determination within the political and legal structures of the nation. This requires imagination, flexibility and, most importantly, political will.

Convention participants unanimously supported a motion for the rights of indigenous people to self-determination, and indicated that it be included in a formal document of reconciliation or by specific provisions of the Constitution or a bill of rights.

Yet self-determination for indigenous people is not only the attainment of the political, civil, economic, social, and cultural rights that white Australians take for granted. Aborigines and Torres Strait Islanders view the quest for self-determination and land rights as one and the same struggle. Josie Crawshaw of ATSIC (Aboriginal and Torres Strait Islander Commission) declares that Aboriginal sovereignty was never ceded to the British and land rights are a prerequisite for reconciliation. Henrietta Fourmile of the Rainforest Aboriginal Network says that introduced land-use and management practices have wrought massive environmental damage, and the Aboriginal quest for land rights and reconciliation is motivated not only by the need for spiritual and physical survival, but also by a cultural imperative to care for country—to nurse it back to health again. Olga Havenan of the Central Land Council fears self-determination is slipping away as a result of the current debate over indigenous land rights. With it, she declares, goes any possibility of reconciliation.

A number of international visitors to the convention gave presentations affirming the importance of self-determination in the reconciliation process. Ted Moses, Chief of the Grand Council of the Crees in Quebec, asserts that the whole principle of reconciliation rests on the state's ability to recognize and respect the human rights of indigenous people. Self-determination, he argues, implies sharing the national wealth and is the final test of the sovereign state that has come to terms with its own history and is determined to include all of its peoples in the vision of its own future.

Professor James Anaya, Special Counsel for the Indian Law Resource Center in New Mexico, argues that the principle of self-determination, properly understood, is an animating force for the efforts toward reconciliation with Aboriginal peoples. It requires confronting and reversing the legacies of empire, discrimination, and cultural suffocation. It does so not to condone vengefulness or spite for past evils, or to foster divisiveness, but rather to build a social and political order based on relations of mutual understanding and respect among peoples.

MAKING A NEW START

Jon Altman (Center for Aboriginal Economic Policy Research) argues that any vision for reconciliation must include broad strategies for eliminating the current marginal economic status of indigenous people. On the one hand, he notes, many Australians believe that indigenous people are a financial drain and that they contribute little; on the other, many indigenous people believe that they are denied access to economic opportunities and that historical legacy will never allow them economic equality. Under such circumstances, there is a need to present facts about the extent of current disadvantage. Pragmatic strategies can then be formulated to facilitate the reduction of economic inequality for the betterment of all. Barrie Thomas (Codirector, The Body Shop) brings a sympathetic nuance to this perspective. He stresses that business leaders must turn their eyes from the short-term financial balance sheet and look at the social balance sheet. There is a need to examine who their suppliers are and whether they can use their purchasing power to establish new industries within indigenous communities.

Many non-Aborigines across Australia are making an outstanding effort in providing avenues for Aboriginal participation in the broader community. However, as I demonstrate in the coming chapters, it is the deeply-felt yearning of Aborigines for there to be an equivalent acknowledgment that non-Aborigines owe their livelihood, at a fundamental level, to indigenous people. Mandawuy Yunupingu, Lead Singer of the rock band *Yothu Yindi*, argues that despite much of the feel-good rhetoric Aborigines have heard since 1988—talk of treaties and compacts—overall conditions in which indigenous people live have changed little. A close associate of Elcho Island's David Burrumarra, Mandawuy advocates a policy of membership-and-remembership. Whites must acknowledge and respect Aboriginal ways and share the proceeds of the development of Aboriginal land. Similarly, the Elcho Island leader Djiniyini Gondarra, in his presentation to the Australian Reconciliation Convention, called on non-Aborigines to declare that they stand with Aborigines in their struggle for justice. He said:

> We Aboriginal Australians understand our spiritual connectedness to this land. Christians have an understanding of spirituality, and this is a place we can begin our journey together. I believe that Aboriginal people need to acknowledge that other Australians born of this land have tasted the spirituality of the land, even if they haven't recognized it.

Again this is an example of membership-and-remembership, an ideology of reconciliation commonly espoused in northeast Arnhem Land. Aborigines wish to take advantage of the opportunities presented to them by non-Aborigines, and will do what is required for such participation. But at the same time, non-Aborigines must affirm the privileged place of indigenous people as keepers of the sacred traditions and learn from Aborigines how to properly treat the land and sea. This is the desired balance central to the Arnhem Land philosophy. The Most Rev. Peter Hollingsworth, Anglican Archbishop of Brisbane, is in agreement, noting that a document of reconciliation will celebrate this oneness in diversity and interdependence. It will promote social transformation—the idea of healing and smoothing over past divisions—for making a new start.

4

The Yolngu and Their Dreaming

My objective in the remainder of the text is to highlight the various arguments for reconciliation, in particular the ideology of adoption or membership-and-remembership, as it is understood in the settlement of Galiwin'ku on Elcho Island.[11] I chose this community not because it is the home of film star David Gulpilil of "Walkabout," "Storm Boy," and more recently "Crocodile Dundee" fame, or the immensely popular rock band, *Yothu Yindi*. For a place that is inaccessible by road and closed to the general public, Elcho Island generates a considerable amount of press, in fact way out of proportion to its size. Though living outside of mainstream Australian politics, Elcho Islanders always appear to be present when indigenous news is being generated or discussed. And residents have a way of attracting attention to themselves. In the 1980s there were rallies in support of peace prior to the Gulf War, candle-lit vigils to register disapproval at the Northern Territory's euthanasia legislation, and forty-eight-hour fasts drawing attention to the needs of those in the world less privileged than Aborigines.[12] Yet in many ways Galiwin'ku is typical of many remote Aboriginal settlements throughout Australia. Unemployment levels are high, living conditions are poor, and social problems on the rise. Residents know what they want for the future. They want what is best for themselves, their families, and clan, but what is also true to the past. Yet the Galiwin'ku approach to intercultural

---

11. Elcho Island was named by the explorer Howard in honor of Scotland's Lord Elcho, who distinguished himself in the Caribbean in the 1700s. Grid reference is 11 degrees, 58 minutes south; 135 degrees, 43 minutes west.

12. A snake ceremony was orchestrated by Galpu clan members upon Elvis Presley's death. Elvis was assigned membership of the Galpu clan because his gyrating hips resembled the dance movement associated with the snake, a Galpu totem.

relations contrasts strongly with that of neighboring Arnhem Land communities. By living and working in this part of the Northern Territory for seven years in the 1980s and 1990s, I became aware that Elcho Islanders posit the Dreaming—that body of ancient lore relevant to all times and states of being—as the source of inspiration for their reconciliatory endeavors.

What does the idea of reconciliation mean to Aborigines in this part of the world at this specific point in their history? Galiwin'ku residents are pursuing equitable partnerships in mining ventures, joint management strategies for resource exploitation in the Arafura Sea, and a treaty (or its equivalent) which affirms their right to self-determination. The goal of Elcho Island elders is to make this vision a reality, but they know that they are largely at the mercy of a voting public that disagrees with what it means to raise one's hand in support of indigenous people.

CHAPTER OUTLINES

My case studies focus attention on the political activities and aspirations of one clan group at Elcho Island, the Warramiri. This clan, more than others, has actively pursued reconciliation for the past forty years. For its leaders, this has entailed (1) the uniting of Aboriginal and Christian beliefs, (2) the attempt to find recognition for Aboriginal rights within the wider Australian community, and (3) the achievement by Aborigines of a level of wealth comparable to that of other Australians through utilization of the land and sea via mining, tourism, and fishing ventures.

During the bicentennial in 1988, members of the Warramiri clan put forward a plan for the creation of a series of new Australian flags which would represent the partnership they envisaged as being essential for Australia's future. The flags would combine both Aboriginal and non-Aboriginal symbols relevant to the area in which they were flying. One Warramiri flag, for instance, combined whale and octopus insignia, reflecting the fact that Warramiri land was the product of the creational activities of these Dreaming figures, and the Union Jack. Wherever one travels in Australia, the leader David Burrumarra asserted, one must respect the powers inherent in the land, both Aboriginal and non-Aboriginal.

Members of the Warramiri clan also initiated a plan for the joint management of the Arafura Sea, which lies between Australia and Indonesia. In this water, the Aborigines believe, are sacred totems, song cycles, ceremonies, and the pathways of creational beings. The aim of the plan was to see both Aboriginal and non-Aboriginal knowledge combined in the management of the sea and for the Warramiri and other Aborigines to progressively reassume responsibility for various levels of its care, based on customary law. Ideas such as this and the flag, I argue, are fundamental to the northeast Arnhem Land concept of reconciliation.

Unlike most other Australian Aboriginal groups, northeast Arnhem Landers had prior experience with non-Aborigines before the arrival of colonizers and missionaries in the twentieth century. Bugis, Macassarese, and Sama-Bajau (sea gypsies), collectively known as Macassans, from what is now known as Sulawesi in Indonesia, established trading relations with the Warramiri and other clans at least 200 years before the arrival of Europeans. Macassans came in search of the exotic delicacy trepang, which was sold at great profit to the Chinese, making this trade Australia's first international industry. Aborigines cooperated with the visitors in the collection and processing of the seafood and, in return for their labor, received metals, cloth, and tobacco. This contact, it is speculated, has allowed the northeast Arnhem Land Aborigines to better deal with the onset of rapid social change that came in the wake of the arrival of "missionaries, miners and misfits" in the twentieth century. The memory of this contact is examined in the context of its relevance to the way Warramiri now press for the recognition of their rights in the broader Australian community.

In the remainder of this book, chapters are broadly in two sections: setting the scene and outlining the relevance of the Dreaming in the reconciliation process. In this chapter the Aborigines of northeast Arnhem Land (Yolngu) and the traditional land-based Aboriginal religion known as the Dreaming or Wangarr are introduced. I then examine the range of ways in which northeast Arnhem Landers are accommodating, and finding accommodation in, mainstream society. Chapter 6 describes the impact of the Warramiri on the cause for reconciliation since the 1950s, and Chapter 7 highlights the Dreaming narratives of Birrinydji, for traditional ideas relating to reconciliation provide many of the older generation with a framework for contemporary negotiations with non-Aborigines. The vision of Warramiri clan leader David Burrumarra of new flags for the nation, for instance, has its origin in narratives of first contact with non-Aborigines. In Chapters 8 to 11, I provide illustrations of Aboriginal initiative aimed at achieving a rapprochement with non-Aborigines. I introduce the voices of a new generation of Galiwin'ku residents and Warramiri, and examine the following issues:

- self-determination and the Galiwin'ku Black Crusade
- the joint management of sea resources between the Australian government, the Indonesian government, and Aboriginal people
- Aborigines, the mining industry, and the power of veto over development
- celebrating through dance, a shared history with Macassans

ELCHO ISLANDERS AND THEIR LAND

Arnhem Land is very low lying and, as one travels east from Darwin, the coast is lined with crocodile-infested mangroves. Elcho Island, however, marks a transition to deep water and sandy beaches. Although the channel between the island and the mainland is largely muddy, coastal waters are clear and abound in sea life, supplying a majority of Yolngu with the greater part of their diet.

Elcho Island is about 60 kilometers long and only a few kilometers wide. It is covered by open forest and is generally flat. The unpopulated interior is dotted with red sand dunes, an indicator of the fact that just a few thousand years ago the coastline was several hundred kilometers further out to sea, and the present community living area was a part of the arid Australian outback. The settlement of Galiwin'ku is situated on a lone hilltop, the eagle's nest in Aboriginal mythology, on a beautiful and natural Arafura Sea harbor. The community was originally centered on a freshwater spring, but it soon outgrew this site and now covers a much wider area.

The spread of Aborigines over the landscape in traditional or premission times is reflected in miniature at the settlement at Galiwin'ku. The township is divided roughly into designated clan areas. Warramiri men and women, for instance, live at the beach camp, reflecting the fact that they are "saltwater" Dreaming people. They also live with groups into which they traditionally married, that is, the Dhuwa moiety "saltwater" Galpu and "freshwater" Liyagawumirr clans. Others live in Department of Education housing not tied to any one clan area.

A 1990 Christian baptism on the beach at Galiwin'ku.

Murngin, Wulamba, Miwatj, and Yolngu

The people of northeast Arnhem Land are referred to in the anthropological literature as Murngin, Wulamba and Miwatj. They are also known as *Yolngu*, meaning human being, a word these Aborigines use to refer to themselves. The geographic focus of this study is the Yolngu community of Galiwin'ku. The largest settlement in northeast Arnhem Land, Galiwin'ku was established in 1942 by the Methodist Overseas Mission. Home to approximately 1500 out of a total Yolngu population of 5000, Galiwin'ku is the traditional homeland of the Liyagawumirr clan. They share their country with eleven closely related clans whose territory lies in the immediate vicinity of Elcho Island.

The traditional Aboriginal owners of northeast Arnhem Land are also landowners in the eyes of the Australian law. Aboriginal property rights came under the national spotlight in the 1960s, when Yirrkala Yolngu challenged Nabalco, the Swiss multinational mining corporation, in the Northern Territory court to determine who owned the bauxite-laden Gove peninsula sacred to the memory of Wudal and innumerable other Dreaming entities. As mentioned in Chapter 2, this land-rights case marked the beginning of a movement for indigenous land rights throughout Australia. Yolngu wanted to participate in negotiations, to be able to delineate areas that, due to their sacred nature, would be off-limits to mining. They wanted also to benefit materially from the new mining venture. As is well documented,[13] the court ruled that although Yolngu belonged to the land, it did not belong to them. Justice Blackburn had been sympathetic to the Aboriginal cause, but he was bound by precedent. The law did not recognize community or group land interests, and Blackburn determined that Aboriginal property rights had been wiped out by the British assertion of sovereignty in 1788.[14] The decision of the court prompted the establishment of a commission of inquiry into granting land rights to Aborigines in the Northern Territory (Woodward 1974), leading to the enactment of the Aboriginal Land Rights (Northern Territory) Act 1976, and the formation of land councils to pursue land claims on behalf of traditional Aboriginal landowners and to act as liaison with regard to development proposals.

In 1998, Aborigines made up 25 percent of the Northern Territory's population, and owned more than 50 percent of its land mass. The form of title is inalienable or Aboriginal freehold (fee simple). Indigenous people hold title not just for themselves but for future generations. The land cannot be sold or given away. Nowhere else in

---

13. See Williams 1986.
14. This decision was overturned in the seminal Mabo High Court case in 1991.

Australia do indigenous people have such security of tenure or control over development.

THE DREAMING

Traditional Yolngu law is similar to that practiced by other Australian Aborigines in that the people follow a framework of beliefs and customs established in the Dreaming. The English expression "the Dreaming" is drawn from the central Australian Aranda Aboriginal expression *Altjiringa,* meaning "to see the eternal," for Aborigines believe that they are in touch with fundamental truths while asleep. In Yolngu matha (northeast Arnhem Land languages) the term for the Dreaming is *Wangarr.*[15] It refers to the period when the world was created, the responsible creational beings, and the framework of laws guiding Aboriginal action. Much has been written on the nature of the Dreaming. The most famous Australian writer on the subject of Aboriginal religion is the late Bill Stanner who, along with Ronald Berndt, worked as an anthropological consultant for Yolngu in the Gove land-rights case. On the subject of the Dreaming, Stanner (1958: 225) wrote:

> A central meaning of the Dreaming is that of a sacred, heroic time long ago when men and nature came to be as they are…. The Dreaming concerns the great marvels—how all the fire and water in the world [was] stolen and recaptured; how men made a mistake over sorcery and now have to die from it; how the hills, rivers and water holes were made; how the sun, moon, and stars were set upon their courses.
>
> [It also]…tells how certain things were instituted for the first time—how animals and men diverged from a joint stock that was neither one nor the other; how such social divisions as tribes, clans and language groups were set up; how spirit children were first placed in the water-holes.
>
> [The Dreaming is a]…kind of commentary…on what is thought to be permanent and ordained at the very basis of the world and life…. [It is]…a charter of absolute validity in answer to all questions of why and how. [It is]…a philosophy in the garb of a verbal literature…and is proof that [Aborigines] share two attributes which have largely made human history what it is. The first of these [is]…the metaphysical gift…the ability to transcend oneself, to make acts of imagination so that one can stand "outside"…oneself and

---

15. I use the expression "the Dreaming" throughout this book.

turn the universe and one's fellows into objects of contemplation. The second ability is a drive to try and make sense out of human experience and to find some purpose in the whole human situation.

When I use the term "the Dreaming" in this book, it is not so much in reference to the creation of the world, but as a set of sacred beliefs that provide a commentary on the world and how to act in any given situation. Much of this book is concerned with how the Dreaming comes into play when Aborigines in northeast Arnhem Land consider the subject of reconciliation. Dreaming beliefs are imprinted upon a whole series of totems and ancestral beings, but when Aboriginal people use the expression "the Dreaming" they are often referring to *all* ancestral entities relevant to their personal and clan history. For example, one may refer to the Octopus Dreaming when comtemplating the legacy of this totemic being in a given area or social situation, and to "the Dreaming" when considering the legacy of all sacred entities—in other words, to Aboriginal law or *Rom*. According to Warramiri Aboriginal leader David Burrumarra, it is as teenagers that Yolngu come to understand the events of the Wangarr (or creation period). They do this by performing songs and ceremonies handed down through the generations, and by being shown tangible reminders of the travels of Dreaming beings. Burrumarra said that when the world was being shaped into its present form, the totemic cuttlefish Nyunyul rose up from the deep waters to create the island of Yumaynga for Warramiri Yolngu to dwell upon. Members of the clan honor this Dreaming and observe strict taboos regarding the consumption of its flesh. Initiated members of the clan have the responsibility to perform rituals for such Dreaming entities, and they fashion ceremonial objects or *rangga* in their likeness to activate life-sustaining powers. Such beings also provide the practical knowledge necessary to support everyday life, such as the ability to hunt, fish, or prepare otherwise toxic foods important to the Aboriginal diet. The flesh of the hawksbill turtle, another Warramiri totem, contains poison glands which must be carefully removed prior to eating. Warramiri Yolngu from the youngest age are familiar with this technique.

As Yolngu grow older, they accumulate more and more of the essence of the totems, which the Dreaming entities bequeathed to them. At death, the souls of clan members go to reside within the sacred water hole, also a place from which spirit-children emerge to create new generations. For Warramiri Yolngu, for example, the souls of the dead go to sacred water holes at Dholtji, Nangingburra, and MataMata, but also to an island paradise well to the north of Arnhem Land, traveling there on the back of the whale. The sacred water hole is the dwelling place of the major totemic Dreamings, and any disturbance is regarded as potentially dangerous for the future of a population. If a sacred site is violated, sickness might befall a clan member, or there might be an earthquake or floods.

Change in the Yolngu World

Aborigines claim to speak with authority about the land and sea and everything connected with it because the rules they follow are said to have been laid down once and for all at the "beginning of time." The laws of the Dreaming are unlike those that Yolngu see enforced in regional courthouses or enacted at sittings of the state and federal houses of Parliament. Non-Aboriginal law is perceived as being constantly prone to change and, almost by definition, discriminatory toward indigenous peoples. Aboriginal law, by contrast, is viewed as fundamentally unchanging and just.

Contemporary approaches to anthropology treat culture and tradition as inherently dynamic and changing. Local understandings are framed by both historical circumstances and particular social contexts. Culture is a contemporary human product rather than a passively inherited legacy (e.g., Linnekin 1992:249). Such understandings have brought some anthropologists and Aborigines into conflict in recent times. This is particularly true in the Northern Territory where large mining companies advocating that Aborigines pay their own way have taken issue with the "invention of tradition" school of anthropological thought and employed consultants to investigate why so many Aboriginal sacred sites coincide with the largest deposits of accessible and exportable minerals. While Aborigines acknowledge that new knowledge is constantly being revealed in dreams, in premonitions, and via cultural diffusion, they are critical of the way anthropologists depict their way of life. Marika-Mununggiritj (1991:22), a Yolngu from Yirrkala, declares:

> ... When the [*Balanda*, or non-Aborigines] came here they had the privilege of learning about our life. But they wrote it down and recorded it as if it were from a fairy tale, as if it were dead.... Yolngu knowledge is living, and it comes from a real world, it has real life.... That's what happens with the old ancestral stories, we still relive that past history, we still sing it, dance and still bring it and fit it into the present.

While Elcho Island Yolngu profess there to have been no change in Aboriginal religion since the beginning of time, a majority identify themselves as Christian, and the relationship between presently popular fundamentalist beliefs and traditional totemic and ancestral beliefs is the subject of much local debate. The local adoption of Christianity at Galiwin'ku has come hand in hand with a desire by Aborigines to be united with Balanda under a set of laws having their foundation in the Dreaming. For instance, in the Adjustment Movement in Arnhem Land in 1957, there had been a "changing of

Genesis" (the Dreaming) to allow a place for such new beliefs in the Aboriginal world view.

But the efforts to achieve such a reconciliation of beliefs have been dogged by the intellectual challenge of pursuing the religion of domineering non-Aborigines. The major struggle for Elcho Island Christians has been to allow a place for Christianity, and thereby build a relationship with non-Aborigines, but also to achieve a sense of continuity with the past. In a sermon in July 1992, for example, the Aboriginal Minister Mawunydjil Garrawirritja asked the congregation, "When did the Good News first come to Arnhem Land?" Some people said it came with the missionaries, but then the Minister said, "But God has always been here, preparing our minds and bodies for the message." Another Christian Minister from Elcho Island, Rronang Garrawurra (1982:4) in a similar way, writes,

> Before the white man came, God revealed Himself, to show that He is God. He chose our ancestors and showed them how to make a Law. This was passed on from generation to generation until now. We remember our sacred areas because of this.

Aborigines from all clan groups at Elcho Island have stories associating Christianity with their own group's cultural heritage, and in the 1990s, the Bible has become an essential part of the Dreaming. As Bos (1988) argues:

> The Dreaming is expressed in symbolic thought; in symbols which are multivocal and open-ended, and therefore open to different interpretations and adjustment. What Aboriginal culture does is to embrace "an ideology of non-change"...but ...this is not at all the same thing as regarding The Dreaming as unchanged, unchanging and unchangeable....
>
> Aboriginal people protect and uphold the unquestioned and final authority of The Dreaming as the foundation of human existence and the basis for personal meaning structures ...this in no way precludes an ability to come to grips with new experienced realities...[which] come to be regarded as emanating from the supernatural beings... (Bos 1988:435)

YOLNGU SOCIAL STRUCTURE

Overview

A pervasive dualism structures the Yolngu universe. Depending on the moiety of the father, a person is born into one of two moieties, named Dhuwa or Yirritja. Yolngu social organization requires that Dhuwa marry Yirritja, so a family unit is usually comprised of a mother of one moiety, and her husband and children of the opposite moiety. Unlike before mission times, today at Elcho Island there are twelve resident clan groups, six of which are Dhuwa and six Yirritja. The Mala or clan is the most significant element of the Yolngu social universe. Clan identity refers to common rights in Dreaming songs, designs, and ceremonies. Members claim rights of access to knowledge in such matters, and male elders carefully control its access and distribution. An individual obtains his or her clan identity through the father, but each individual also has "native title" interests in the land of his mother and his mother's mother.

A map of clan territories in northeast Arnhem Land will show the land to be divided up as in a checkerboard manner, giving an impression of distinct bands of people once spread evenly over the landscape. But this is an erroneous impression. Social interaction in north-east Arnhem Land entails a "...structure of overlapping, interlocking, and open social networks rather than a segmentary structure of clearly defined groups" (Keen 1994:63). Both Dhuwa and Yirritja clans are associated with the coastal zone reefs and islands; areas where the coast is dotted with muddy creeks and mangrove trees; and inland, where the emu and big red kangaroo roam and fresh water is a scarce commodity. Similar living environments do not equate with similar beliefs, however. Dhuwa and Yirritja doctrines concerning origins are entirely different.

Clan members are reminded of the importance of living together in harmony by merely surveying the land and seascape. The trees, birds, fish and animals, all the things that make up the natural world belong to one of the moieties. A Dhuwa moiety stringy-bark gum tree stands alongside a Yirritja ironbark gum in the open field, as do Yirritja paper bark trees and Dhuwa bulrushes in the freshwater swamps, reflecting the fact that the world is made up of these inter-marrying pairs. Similarly, the strikingly colored Dhuwa moiety parrot fish and the Yirritja crayfish both dwell amongst the coral beds, and both may be objects of desire for the hunter.

The Mythological Basis

The system whereby Yolngu clans relate to one another within a moiety has its foundation with the Dreaming figures Lany'tjun for the Yirritja moiety and Djang'kawu for the Dhuwa moiety. They showed Yolngu how to live together by establishing a pattern of kinship that both moieties share. The Warramiri clan, for example, are related to other Yirritja clans as either maari (maternal grandparent) to gutharra (maternal grandchild), or as waawa (brother) etc. This patterning of relations is fundamental to the Yolngu concept of membership-and-remembership, as I will describe later.

Both Lany'tjun and Djang'kawu ascribe to each clan certain totemic affiliations, bodies of law and a language. For the Yirritja moiety, clan totems are associated with the sandfly, honeybee, the cycad, crocodile, and so on. Lany'tjun and Djang'kawu are deemed to have initiated the use of ritual objects and specific designs in artwork by Yolngu. They provided land rights for their respective groups and introduced various land management techniques. But Lany'tjun and Djang'kawu are also fundamentally different. Yolngu credit Djang'kawu with the creation of certain natural species and human populations, while Lany'tjun is remembered more for his social and ceremonial innovations.

When the Djang'kawu came to Arnhem Land, the world had already been "hatched" from an egg they released into the void. The land was divided from the sea and sky, and birds, fish, and all the animals that are here today were present. But there were no people. Into this world came two sisters and a brother (collectively known as Djang'kawu), who set about populating the uninhabited lands with Dhuwa moiety peoples. With the rising sun, they came to Yolngu territory in a sailing canoe from the island of Bralgu, out of the sea in the east. Dolphins swam alongside and black crows flew overhead showing the way. In each place they visited, the Djang'kawu sisters stuck their yam digging sticks into the earth, creating freshwater springs. Then they let children out from their wombs, giving each new set a homeland, totemic markers, and rituals to perform.

Elcho Island is a major sacred site for Djang'kawu. Galiwin'ku, in one of its meanings, refers to the "left arm" of this creator. It was here that the very first circumcision was performed on a Yolngu, and a rock in the sea represents the foreskin that "flew off" after the operation. Djang'kawu gave the name *Nyoka* to the mud crab at this location and made it a totem for the landowning Liyagawumirr clan. Djang'kawu also left on the beach, in the form of a sacred rock, an emblem of the sun, which symbolizes the Dhuwa moiety. "Unity in diversity" could be a motto for the Djang'kawu legacy. The Liyagawumirr, like all other Dhuwa clans, are in possession of totems specific to them alone, but they also have access to emblems that unite the Dhuwa moiety as a whole. When Djang'kawu departed from Galiwin'ku, they headed to the west, always with the rising sun, where they performed more miraculous feats and laid a foundation of unity for clans the length and breadth of Arnhem Land.

The story of Lany'tjun is different principally because it does not speculate on Yirritja origins. Yirritja men and women are themselves the children of Dhuwa mothers. In one of his many manifestations, Lany'tjun is a *barramundi*, a much favored table fish. At the beginning of time Lany'tjun could see that the Yolngu were starving and living in fear of one another, so he transformed himself from a *barramundi* into a human in order to teach the people how to survive. He divided the Yirritja Aborigines into a number of clans, each with their own country, and taught them the basics of the religious life. Lany'tjun showed them how to catch fish, and the elusive freshwater turtle, and gave instructions on where to find drinking water in the parched landscape. He united the Yolngu by giving all the Yirritja clans a single ceremony, the *Ngaarra*, to perform. In fact Yolngu say that when the bodies of the assembled men are adorned with Lany'tjun's sacred designs and they execute his ceremony, they are Lany'tjun enacting his decree in the world. There will be peace and an end to hunger and strife between the clans. The impact of Lany'tjun's teachings was revolutionary, but some Yolngu were jealous, and they decided to kill him. Following his slaying, his body was thrown into the lake from which he had emerged. The frogs, long-neck turtles, and barramundi rekindled his spirit, however, and he lived on in a new guise, that of the Dreaming figure Banatja, who taught even more to the Yolngu. In this way, the laws of Lany'tjun spread throughout the land.

YOLNGU, MACASSANS, AND EUROPEANS

Northeast Arnhem Land has been the scene of much contact between Aborigines and non-Aborigines throughout several centuries. In 1642 the Dutchman Abel Tasman traversed the northern coast of "New Holland" as Australia was once known, and British and French explorers did the same in the early 1800s. Myths and legends from the repertoire of coastal Aboriginal clans in northeast Arnhem Land reveal, however, a broader range of contacts. Oral history, as well as narratives from the Dreaming, speak of dark-skinned hunters from the north harpooning and cutting up whales along the coast (Solor Islanders?[16]); golden-skinned sailors with a code of conduct resembling the military (Bugis?[17]); and men with long swords and hats of "mirror" upon their heads and shoulders (Portuguese?). The most extensive contact was with Macassans, and a number of books have been written about Aboriginal experiences with these peoples (e.g., Macknight 1976).

Macassans would arrive every year in November and stay for approximately three months in search of the trepang (the sea cucumber, *Holothuria scabra*), an exotic element of the Chinese diet and a major component of their bride wealth. Seasonal voyages were made from Sulawesi from at least 1700 until 1907, when the arrival of people from the north was prohibited by federal law as part of the country's "white Australia policy." The presence of Macassan fisherfolk in Aboriginal waters still has relevance for Aborigines, for it provided the opportunity to formulate cosmological adaptations, such as the Birrinydji, or "whiteman Dreaming," from which Burrumarra drew for

---

16. The only traditional whale hunters in Indonesia.
17. Eastern Indonesian seafarers.

inspiration in his reconciliatory endeavors. While at once providing an explanation of Aboriginal poverty in relation to non-Aborigines, Birrinydji is also a foundation for widespread Yolngu resistance to western hegemony and is a stimulus for achieving negotiated settlements for land and sea use, as I will explain.

Christian Missions

Yolngu, on the whole, were spared the worst aspects of European contact owing to the remoteness of northeast Arnhem Land. The unsuitability of the land for cattle, local resistance to this industry, and also the establishment of the Arnhem Land Reserve by the federal government in the late 1920s saw most Warramiri living in relative isolation prior to the World War II. Only missionaries, whose activities were concentrated in the coastal settlements of Milingimbi (established in 1923), Yirrkala (1935), and Galiwin'ku, Elcho Island (1942); Japanese pearlers; European beachcombers; and anthropologists were in regular contact with the Aborigines.

The impact of Christian missions on these peoples has been profound, but the policies pursued in northeast Arnhem Land contrasted strongly with those in other areas of Australia (Keen 1994:26–27). Children were not separated from their parents and incarcerated in dormitories, nor were ceremonies banned or people forced to speak English. Many Yolngu freely joined the mission at Galiwin'ku in the 1940s, though not everyone's intention was to become Christian, or even to stay. There was certainly a wish for an end to the strife which plagued relations between the clans, particularly since the departure of Macassans, and a desire for access to cloth and tobacco, among other things. However, there were also millenarian-type expectations. In following church law, Balanda and Yolngu would share equally in the wealth of the land and Yolngu would regain their place as masters of their own destiny.

Within a very short period, the greater part of Arnhem Land became depopulated as people moved into coastal communities. Harold Shepherdson, Galiwin'ku missionary from 1942 until his retirement in the 1980s, was aware of the importance to Aborigines of maintaining strong ties to their sacred places and encouraged as many people as possible to stay on or return to their homelands. Rather than have Aborigines travel to the settlement for supplies of flour, molasses, and tobacco, he would fly these out to where the people had always lived, trading store goods for crocodile skins and artwork.

In the 1950s twelve clans had come together to forge a new life within a single community, but were facing great struggles. These clans had not previously lived together, and rivalry and suspicion threatened the settlement's future. Galiwin'ku is on Dhuwa moiety land belonging to the Liyagawumirr Mala, and traditional etiquette demands that they will lead the community. Yet in the early years of the settlement's existence, the Aboriginal Council supporting the mission was led by members of the Yirritja moiety Wangurri and Warramiri clans. A contemporary report of the Uniting (formerly Methodist) Church suggests that across Arnhem Land, the authority of traditional landowners was being challenged by newly arriving Aborigines of the opposite moiety, a phenomenon almost unheard of in pre-mission times (ARDS 1994).

In 1974, after a short 32 years, the Methodist Church withdrew from direct involvement and control of the mission. Yolngu however were completely unprepared for the change. Those living on missions, perhaps 90 percent of the total Yolngu population, had become totally dependent people (ARDS 1994). One response to the problems of contact with non-Aboriginal society generally was for Yolngu to leave the mission to establish outstations or homelands in their own country. An attempt to evolve a lifestyle which preserved the essence of the Aboriginal way of life along with access to chosen elements from non-Aboriginal society, the homeland movement is flourishing. Galiwin'ku now has over 16 homelands within a 50 kilometer radius of the settlement. Another response by residents was to ensure that the landowners had a predominant say in settlement decision making, that they received compensation or royalties payments for the use of their land, and were guaranteed that planned developments were in accord with Yolngu law.[18] Progress for the Yolngu in the post-mission period has been slow and steady. Galiwin'ku today is an incorporated community, and Yolngu are taking advantage of the greater autonomy this has made possible. Residents continue to reclaim their status as leaders, educators, and health-care providers, utilizing, where possible, the knowledge of their forefathers. As Coombs (1994) says, in the past "Too often they were allowed to act only as passive institutionalized recipients of services, reacting as beneficiaries or victims." Now they are in a position to take an active role as agents in negotiating with federal, state and local governments, as well as with private enterprises which were impinging on their lives. In the 1990s, Yolngu determine the nature and extent of their involvement in Australian society.

WARRAMIRI MALA IDENTITY

The Yirritja Warramiri clan is a population group within a collection of clans referred to by Warner (1958) as the Murngin (Murrnginy). In the

---

18. Both the supply company Barge Express and Telecom must pay traditional owners lease money for the use of land on Elcho Island, even though Aborigines are the beneficiaries of their services.

1920s Warner used this term as a label for both Dhuwa and Yirritja moieties, but in current usage it is of significance only for the Yirritja half of Yolngu society. It was originally defined as "fire sparks" (Warner 1959) or, according to Burrumarra, the sparks that fly as the ironsmith's hammer hits the anvil. For the Warramiri it refers to "people of the iron age" or modern world. Murrnginy is a word that occurs periodically throughout the book, for it provides a key to understanding the traditional Warramiri perspective on reconciliation. The Murrnginy era was ushered in with the "discovery" or uncovering of the laws of the Dreaming figure Birrinydji, who is believed to be the foundation of the material wealth of non-Aborigines.

The word *Warramiri* means "high red cloud" (Cawte 1993:106), and there are two branches in the broader Warramiri Mala. There is Burrumarra's Warramiri-Budalpudal, whose major Dreaming site is Dholtji, and the Warramiri-Mandjikay, who are linked to Matamata and Gawa. The term Warramiri also refers to a *Matha* or language that these Mala groups share. In saying that one is Warramiri, one is referring to membership in a Mala associated with particular Dreaming laws and tracts of land, and that one has access to a language historically used in those areas. From the Pama-Nyungan group, the Warramiri language is not widely spoken and, unlike many of the other Yolngu languages, has not been the subject of detailed linguistic studies. Apart from senior men and women, who are themselves multilingual, most younger Warramiri speak Djambarrpuyngu, which is a lingua franca at Galiwin'ku. This is the language taught in the local school's bilingual program.

All Warramiri members claim common ancestry because of shared beliefs in certain totemic sea species, most notably the whale, octopus, and cuttlefish, and because they possess ritual objects or *rangga* linked to these Dreamings. Unity within the Warramiri clan is strengthened by the fact that a majority of members have the surname Bukulatjpi, which is the name of a historical Warramiri leader who "discovered" Birrinydji at the time of the Macassans.

In the living memory of the senior members of the clan, there used to be other branches of the Warramiri Mala. There was the Wuduymung, the Guku-Warramiri, and the Girrkirr (Rika). Other groups are also known to have preceded these, and there are references to such populations in Warramiri personal names. How and why these clans disappeared is a mystery, though it is acknowledged that clan warfare was continuous in pre-mission times, and that diseases, such as smallpox introduced by Macassans and influenza by Europeans, had devastating consequences.

Warramiri country lies to the north and east of Galiwin'ku, but a majority of clan members moved to the settlement in the 1940s when it became a Methodist Church mission. Warramiri also live at the other coastal communities of Milingimbi and Yirrkala and at outstations at the northern tip of Elcho Island. Major centers in the Warramiri Dreaming, places such as Dholtji and the English Company's Islands, are uninhabited and infrequently visited, although discussions are continuing within the clan to make Dholtji a large settlement with "many fine houses," as Aboriginal history suggests was once the case.

The Warramiri Dreaming is centered on the open sea and coral reef and yet Aboriginal title to land in the Northern Territory extends only as far as the low watermark, a decision based solely on European ideas of what constitutes rights to country. This has brought the Warramiri to the fore in the struggle for native title recognition of sea rights. For coastal and island Aboriginal people throughout Australia, the traditional estate does not end at the shoreline. Dreaming tracks flow out over the seas, forming an indissoluble link to the land (Allen 1994).

In terms of population, about 200 Yolngu identify themselves as Warramiri. This represents a substantial increase from pre-mission days, when the pioneering American anthropologist Lloyd Warner, traversing the area in the late 1920s, suggested that average clan numbers were around fifty, though fluctuating constantly as a result of interclan warfare. A small percentage of Warramiri work in the local school, store, health center, homelands, or as pastors in the church. One Warramiri leader, Terry Yumbulul, was recently employed as the Galiwin'ku town clerk. A majority of clan members either receive a government pension or are involved in a "work for the dole" scheme, called the Community Development Employment Project (CDEP), established by the Commonwealth Government in 1977. Under this scheme, unemployment benefits are pooled and recipients undertake development projects given priority within the community. As Coombs (1994:163) says, "The idea helped Aborigines escape from the fear that the [unemployment or pension] money they received [as is their right as Australian citizens] was an unrequited gift carrying a potential obligation to repay, and to escape from the dependencies of welfare."

A typical middle-aged Warramiri man or woman at Galiwin'ku is employed in the town by CDEP, belongs to a family that owns a dinghy or a four-wheel-drive vehicle, and participates in weekly hunting excursions for either fish or turtle, or kangaroo and goanna on the homelands. The Warramiri maintain three communities, Nyikala, Dholtji, and Yirringa, and each has a garden that supplies fresh fruit and vegetables, like cassava and bananas, for the resident families. New homes are always under construction, and young men learn the skills of the building trade within their home territories. Young women find opportunities for employment at the local store or in the health center or school. The larger homelands have either a small shelter for the purposes of education or a Department of Education classroom equipped with a satellite television and radio or telephone for contact to the hub school.

Life on the homelands is carefree for the young. The open sea is before them, and there is lots of exploring to do; but for adults it is an escape from the pressures of the main community. The average three-bedroom house at Galiwin'ku contains more than twenty people and, as is inevitable with such numbers, is impossible to maintain. With this overcrowding comes other problems, borne by a lack of privacy and personal security. One's possessions are the possession of everyone in the immediate vicinity, and it is only because there is a high level of trust between members of the settlement that the community remains a viable option.

The health of the Yolngu has suffered because of poor living conditions. In fact, it is cause for national concern. Prime Minister John Howard, in a visit to Galiwin'ku in 1998, commented on the situation. The streets are dusty and filled with litter. Asthma, gastrointestinal ailments, and eye problems are endemic. Petrol and glue sniffing is rife among teenagers, and while Galiwin'ku is a "dry" or alcohol-free community, illegally-consumed beer and Fijian kava[19] are destroying family and community life. The word genocide is often used to describe what is happening to the Aboriginal population. Trained Aboriginal health workers work hand in hand with visiting doctors and public-health nurses to improve the living conditions and lives of settlement dwellers, but there is a limit on what they can do. White sugar, white flour, and fatty foods are highly desirable, but they are also a cause of diseases which were unheard of in pre-mission times. Education is often considered a key to finding solutions to these problems, but it is a long-term and uphill battle.

An atmosphere of quiet despair pervades much of the community. Apart from the intense and frequently-held Christian services, lengthy traditional-type funerals, lasting upwards of five days, are the most noticeable feature on the social calendar. New strategies in the fields of health, education, and community development aimed at improving the lot of Aborigines are frequently given trial runs at Galiwin'ku, but Yolngu have their own ways of dealing with their concerns. It is still the case today, for instance, that many parents and students view the schooling system as an instrument of non-Aboriginal power. Children are there to be changed, to unlearn what their kin have taught them. Aboriginal parents want their children to be competent in the white world, but they also value and want their children to value their Aboriginality. One of the most impressive developments has come as a

---

19. Traditional Fijian ritual drink made from the root of the pepper tree, and brought to Arnhem Land by missionaries in the 1970s as a substitute for alcohol.

result of the pressure that Yolngu brought to bear on public-service administrators for a change in the way their children were being educated. In the 1980s, east Arnhem Land schools began a successful campaign for the Aboriginalization of the classroom. The aim was to introduce an Aboriginal curriculum and pedagogic style, and today classes are taught primarily by Aboriginal teachers in Aboriginal languages. A school action group and council provides opportunities for all members of the community to be involved in the education process on a daily basis. In 1992 at Galiwin'ku, a dialect program was initiated by the author who was then employed as teacher–linguist. Twice a week, Warramiri schoolchildren had the opportunity to hear, speak, and write in their own language. This was seen as vital in maintaining cultural traditions.

In the following chapters, other strategies are discussed. The first to be highlighted is the adoption of non-Aborigines into the Yolngu domain, known as membership-and-remembership. I give an overview of the history of Aboriginal adoption of Balanda and discuss the relevance of this strategy in the reconciliation debate. Adoption, I argue, relies on Balanda not treating Aborigines as helpless or powerless individuals, but as people with something to offer the nation. The Yolngu ambition is to try to bridge the gap between Aboriginal and non-Aboriginal lifestyles and forge a united Australia where the rights of Aborigines are acknowledged and respected.

5

Dealing with Outsiders

In an intercultural setting, Aborigines assert their rights as landholders in a number of ways, primarily through the intervention of land councils. These are largely staffed by non-Aborigines operating under the auspices of federal land-rights laws. However, Yolngu culture itself also provides an avenue for adapting to non-Aboriginal lifeways and for forcing non-Aborigines to adapt to Aboriginal ways. Certain influential Balanda, including anthropologists, are adopted into a Yolngu family and groomed to work on behalf of Aborigines in their dealings with intrusive non-Aboriginal government agencies. Adoption affirms the self-worth of the adoptor and also the importance of the Yolngu cultural inheritance. It is often achieved simply through recital of a story of traditional significance, revealing a sacred site, or the gift of an Aboriginal name. Yolngu acknowledge the importance of non-Aboriginal brokerage. Adoption is a very serious process and a declaration to the outside world that Yolngu are a force to be reckoned with. As Collmann (1988: 235) argues, if Aborigines are to control non-Aborigines at all, they must try and bind them within the boundaries of Aboriginal society.

In the days of Macassans, the opportunity to adopt individuals was largely nonexistent. Adoption was impersonal through the Dreaming and via Birrinydji: the entire group of non-Aborigines became associated with the Yirritja moiety. The object of this large-scale embrace was the same as for individuals, however, in that it attempted to affirm the worth of the adopting moiety and provide Aborigines with an avenue for the pursuit of their goals. As I describe in the next and later chapters, this process of adoption is integral to the Yolngu ideology of membership-and-remembrance. The Yolngu world enlarges and changes as clan members interact with and try to manage relations with whites.

So in this chapter I trace the history of adoption of non-Aborigines into Yolngu lives and culture from the days of Macassans to the present. I highlight the fact that membership-and-remembrance has a political and a religious aspect. Adoption is both a bridge into the world of the non-Aborigine and a means of affirming local authority. It is an integral part of the reconciliation process in the Arnhem Land context.

Adoption into the Yolngu World

Those willing to spend extended periods on Elcho Island find the Yolngu to be very accommodating. A visitor who remains for a few months or longer, if accepted by the community, may be offered a place in the moiety, the clan and kinship system, and in some cases given a personal name. Up until that time, however, the visitor remains a stranger, feeling very alone, even in the midst of a bustling community. If the visitor is given a title, for example brother to an Aboriginal man, then all the people the Aboriginal man calls brother, which include his father's brothers' sons and, in some cases, his mother's sisters' sons, will also call him by the title *waawa* or brother. Suddenly a world opens up, and everyone knows who the visitor really is, and the only barrier to communication is that determined by the kinship system itself. For instance, the visitor must avoid "poison" relations. People classified as mother-in-law or her brothers, and the mother-in-law's mother, will refer to the adoptee as *gurrung* and shun all contact. The only time the *gurrung* is permitted to show affection for a person of the "wrong skin" is upon the "poisoned" one's death. The *gurrung* will direct funeral proceedings and handle the body of the deceased when all others must keep their distance.

Once accepted into a Yolngu family, the visitor is treated as a child who has to be shown the way. But one advances quickly through adolescence to adulthood, where there are certain obligations and responsibilities to fulfill. Yolngu adopt non-Aborigines into their clan for a whole range of reasons. Having a Balanda friend means having access to a world apart from the one of their birth, a place that they can travel to and learn about, for there is much curiosity about life in the larger cities of Australia. The adoptee is expected to discharge a number of functions, such as defender of the Yolngu when impersonal government agencies are threatening some aspect of their life, for example cutting off a pension check; or mediator, when there is a need to speak with a doctor about an illness; or driver, for transportation to and from the airport or to a favorite hunting ground. Through adoption, Yolngu wish to have others understand and affirm the importance of their way of life and values. Expanding the Yolngu ties of kinship is viewed as a ready means of achieving this (Morphy 1983). The more authority that the adoptee wields in the non-Aboriginal world, the higher their status in the Yolngu world. A fighter for Aboriginal rights, a church leader, or a medical specialist is considered a person of great standing in the Yolngu community and is treated accordingly.

Official Visitors

On any particular day, public servants and contractors arrive at the Galiwin'ku airport on regularly scheduled 12-seater Cessnas. They are representatives of ATSIC (the body which replaced the NACC and Department of Aboriginal Affairs), parole officers, education and health department professionals, the Department of Local Government, the Northern Land Council, and so on. Such visits are not coordinated, and Galiwin'ku residents are overwhelmed with meetings. A class of full-time negotiators is emerging in the community to handle the situation—typically council members or older unemployed men and women. Overnight visitors to the island are housed in a fenced-off compound away from the major community living areas.

The fact-finding missions of public servants rarely have an impact on Yolngu lives, and Yolngu know it. They resent the fact that Aboriginal industry employs far more non-Aborigines than indigenous Australians. Many Yolngu see the whole exercise of consultation as a waste of their time and money. Funding set aside for work in Aboriginal Affairs is money that Yolngu "allow" public servants to administer on their behalf. It is as if they are silent and largely unwilling partners in the enterprise. Yolngu permit entry for the public servant, approve the writing of a report they will never see, and live in vain hope of seeing the end of this continued nuisance, or "humbug," as it is called. Often however, the public servant will try to wield power over and above that which Yolngu bestow, and in such cases the permit of entry is revoked.

Yolngu enforce the rules with subtlety. They understand that the rights they enjoy under non-Aboriginal law are intended to mimic the powers they once held under traditional Aboriginal law. Under traditional *Rom* (law), people are loath to create a situation of disharmony, and in the case of an outsider, would rather turn a blind eye to minor breaches of etiquette, dismissing it as ignorance, than create a scene. But in some cases, sterner action is required. The occasional visitor does not always understand and may be resentful if traditional law is applied and and they are banished from the community.

RECONCILIATION AND THE VISITOR

The world has come to Galiwin'ku in recent years in the form of overseas delegations, politicians, and rock musicians. In 1991, Sisters of Charity from Caanan in Germany paid a visit to Elcho Island. According to the Order's head, Mother Baselea, they were on a mission of reconciliation. The previous year the Sisters had been to Israel and, on behalf of Germanic peoples, apologized to Jews for World War Two. In Australia, it was their intention to apologize to the Aborigines (and all indigenous people) for the crimes of white people, and they chose Galiwin'ku as the site of their performance. In a small ceremony by the sea, the sisters prayed for forgiveness, and, in a spirit of reconciliation, the Elcho Island Minister Mowanydjil also asked for absolution. Aborigines carry with them very bad feelings towards the Balanda, the Minister said, and the desire was to let this bitterness go.

Old missionaries have visited the island in the past ten years and have been greeted with a generosity of spirit that is somewhat difficult to comprehend, given the association of the church with Australia's colonization. The year 1992, for instance, was the fiftieth anniversary of the establishment of the mission at Galiwin'ku. Present at the weekend celebrations were many of the settlement workers from the early days. It was a moving, though at times controversial reunion. For instance, in a short play presented for the entertainment of the visitors, Aboriginal Minister Dr. Djiniyini Gondarra dressed as a missionary and acted out his memories of the food rationing days of the 1940s and 1950s. He wore a large hat and carried a stick. In a booming voice, he told the Aboriginal men to line up for their rations, which in this case was a cup of flour, a cup of molasses and some tobacco. One by one he admonished the men for either not coming to church or not working hard enough during the week and, on this basis, distributed or withheld rations. The Aborigines in the audience were delighted with the performance and roared with laughter. The missionaries looked on quietly, unsure of how to respond.

Of particular note were the evening prayer meetings led by the local congregation. On the opening Friday night, Djiniyini called for the missionaries to come forward and to pray the way the Aborigines now do, following a charismatic style. Of the hundreds of visitors, no-one came forward. On the second night, only Harold Shepherdson, the Elcho pioneer, and a few others joined in the circle of prayer. On the last day, the Minister berated the non-Aboriginal audience, saying,

> In the old days we followed you. We kept our heads down because we were ashamed. Now we walk with our heads up and we look at you in the eye and say, "We can be brothers and sisters together." You must pray the way that we do. Come forward.

Virtually all the visitors came forward, joining hands with the Aboriginal congregation.

Apart from meetings of a religious order, there are the occasional visits of politicians of national standing, such as the governor general, the queen's representative in Australia, or the prime minister. Proceedings are somewhat different in such cases. When Aborigines greet outsiders on a spiritual plane, Christianity provides the framework for the coming together. Politicians, however, need to be reminded that in this part of Arnhem Land, you must not only pray the way Aborigines do, but also follow Aboriginal law. There was such a case in February 1998, when Australia's Prime Minister John Howard made a rare trip to Aboriginal land on his way to Papua New Guinea and Malaysia for official visits. As I describe, Yolngu were at pains to impress upon the national leader that reconciliation has both a religious and a political dimension.

The Prime Minister's Visit

A newspaper report dated February 28, 1998 in *The Australian*, the national daily, was headlined "Secret political business in the Top End." It read:

> John Howard took part in a secret Aboriginal ceremony on remote Elcho Island emerging with a self-declared deeper understanding of the ritual and culture of thousands of years of indigenous tradition. Making his first trip to an Aboriginal community after two years as Prime Minister, Mr. Howard was greeted by Elcho people with generous hospitality. As part of his special greeting, the Prime Minister was taken to a secret place for men and was treated to a ceremony that lasted for more than half an hour. In accordance with custom, he had to remove his shoes and sit on the ground. In light rain, Mr. Howard emerged bedecked in orange feathers. As a final step in the process, Mr. Howard placed the feathered item on a ceremonial pole.

I doubt if even the prime minister knew the meaning of the ceremony or "process" in which he participated. The act of taking the leader of the Australian government through a sacred ceremony harks back to the days of the Gove land-rights case, when Yolngu leaders at Yirrkala showed Justice Blackburn sacred *rangga* and *madayin* in an attempt to impress upon him that Aborigines were the landowners who had to be consulted on matters to do with the land and sea. While Blackburn was sympathetic, he stood by an interpretation of law which continued to hold sway until overruled by the Mabo judgment. Repeating history, Howard told reporters at the conclusion of his visit that while he was deeply touched by the Aboriginal ceremonies he had witnessed, it had not changed his fundamental view on the government's Native Title Amendment Bill. However the Yolngu had an agenda more wide ranging in scope than was superficially apparent.

By showing the prime minister the sacred site of the clan and bringing him into the inner sanctum of ceremonial life, Yolngu honor him in ways that only traditional leaders sometimes are honored. By displaying such respect, the Yolngu expect to be shown respect as landowners, as occurs when people are adopted into a family and Mala. Indeed, as part of his tour of nearby Yirrkala, the national leader was greeted by rows of ceremonially dressed men carrying spears and covered in white ochre, and was presented with a petition for Aboriginal customary law to be recognized by Australian law. For Yolngu, the aim of "the process" referred to by the journalist is the creation of a new sense of community, one in which there is an acknowledgment by government of Yolngu traditions and aspirations—and of making the future coincide with visions of how things were in an ideal past.

The prime minister was very moved by his visit to Yolngu lands. *The Australian* reports that he said, "I have never experienced anything like that before. I have always respected Aboriginal culture. But until today I don't think I had understood the depth of feeling the indigenous people have in relation to their culture." But there was to be no Damascus-like conversion on land rights, the report said. The generosity of spirit at Galiwin'ku and Yirrkala had impressed him, but he still believed there was a generosity of spirit on both sides and that native title amendments were a fair compromise between the needs of pastoralists, miners, and Aborigines.

THE CHANGING NATURE OF INTERACTION

The Warramiri Leaders

While Yolngu are now reasonably comfortable with their position as landowners, and appear willing to assert their rights under the Land Rights Act with confidence, things were very different fifty years ago when the mission was first established. Every task in traditional Aboriginal society is performed within guidelines set down in the Dreaming. One's moiety, clan, and *gurrutu* (kinship) determines the individual's many roles. While the social impact of the non-Aboriginal presence has been relatively uniform along the northeast Arnhem Land coast, the role of determining policy on relationships with non-Aborigines was once the sole province of Yolngu of the Yirritja moiety. Members of Yirritja clans such as the Warramiri and Gumatj experienced more intense and prolonged contact with Macassans than other Aborigines, and their leaders played a pivotal role in negotiating trade between the visitors and Aboriginal clans in the hinterland. The belief in a Dreaming being in the figure of a white male, which was "uncovered" in the Macassan period, set the tone for both efforts to resist the undesirable consequences of contact, and also attempts to find accommodation in the new world that was only now being opened to Yolngu.

In the mid-1800s, it was the Warramiri leader Bukulatjpi who was the first to "discover" the Dreaming law associated with the Macassans, the law of Birrinydji, and pass on its meaning to others. Bukulatjpi's descendants, Yamaliny, Lela, Bambung, and Ganimbirrngu, were all "frontmen" or brokers in the days of the Macassans. Ganimbirrngu was referred to by the trepangers as the Last Rajah of Melville Bay, as a mark of his status amongst the Yolngu. Bukulatjpi's progeny all had Macassan names, were followers of the law of Birrinydji and, consequently, were staunch defenders of their lands against unwelcome intrusion or breaches of etiquette.

Ganimbirrngu's son, David Burrumarra, was born in 1917, ten years after the end of the trepang era and 18 years before the establishment of a mission presence near Warramiri territory. For Burrumarra, the Birrinydji "whiteman" Dreaming (shown in the photograph on the book cover) inspired strategies for survival in the difficult times ahead. Through his interpretations, this Dreaming narrative was a foundation for his belief in Christianity, the moral basis for the realization of land and sea rights, and the rationale for a treaty or pact of reconciliation between Aborigines and non-Aborigines. Custodianship of the laws of Birrinydji was tantamount to having a mandate for asserting one's rights in relation to non-Aborigines, and the mediating role that Burrumarra had inherited was taken very seriously in the mission context. Burrumarra led the Aboriginal Council at Galiwin'ku for many years from the 1960s until the 1980s, even though he was not a member of the land owning clan. While over the years many Yolngu questioned his leadership style, few doubted his ritual authority.

Today, however, the situation is different. There has been a transformation in Yolngu politics and the way that Yolngu as a whole deal with non-Aborigines. As I discuss throughout this book, Warramiri Yolngu utilize a two-pronged approach: (1) the traditional outlook, which we can refer to as an "inside" or Dreaming perspective, and (2) political action in accordance with provisions of the Aboriginal Land Rights (Northern Territory) Act 1976 and the Native Title Act 1993. The former holds, for instance, that Warramiri are brokers in terms of relationships with non-Aborigines, but also that Galiwin'ku is Dhuwa land and Dhuwa control everything on it. The latter says that Dhuwa moiety and other affected peoples will be consulted by the government when questions of development arise. They will arrange the agenda for visiting dignitaries or make demands on the non-Aboriginal government for changes in policy toward indigenous rights. This represents a sharp contrast with the early years of the mission, when the Yirritja moiety alone bore the responsibility.

ABORIGINES, MACASSANS, MISSIONARIES AND POLITICIANS

In the days of trepang, a few Yolngu of both moieties would make the annual voyage from Elcho Island to Macassar when the praus returned to the northwest on the trade winds. Yolngu would stay for a year or longer, though some never returned, either lost at sea, taken into slavery by pirates, or marrying and raising a family in Sulawesi or Timor. Those who did return brought back vivid descriptions of the treatment of Indonesians by Dutch colonials and exotic stories of life in seaports like Ujung Pandang (Macassar), Djakapurra (Singapore), or Dobo (Aru). There is no question of the awe in which these places were held, so wealthy did their inhabitants appear. Every young man dreamt of sailing to the north.

As I detail in Chapter Seven, the Yolngu perceived a connection between the wealth of Macassar and the fact that each year for more than two hundred years, a flotilla in excess of forty boats or praus would arrive in Arnhem Land in search of trepang, pearlshell, turtle shell, and sandalwood. On the Australian coast, Warramiri Yolngu like Ganimbirrngu (Burrumarra's father) would assist the fishermen and would have pearls for trade stashed in caves in anticipation of their arrival. Ganimbirrngu would also advise his male children to help the visitors collect the sea floor–dwelling trepang, and to make friends with the Macassans, so they would remember them with gifts on future visits. The Warramiri would dance and celebrate the receipt of trade goods from the visitors, for at the end of the season, the Macassans often presented Yolngu with dug-out sailing canoes and other items. The Warramiri would sing in honor of the Dreaming being that was understood to be the original source of goods now found to be indispensable, such as knives, cloth, tobacco, and so on. A magical or spiritual origin was attributed to them, and the only reason why Macassans and the Dutch possessed such wealth was because they had access to Aboriginal land and the proceeds of the "whiteman" Dreaming being Birrinydji. This Dreaming figure, however, was associated with Yirritja clans like the Warramiri, Gumatj, Dhalwangu, and they alone were the rightful heirs to Birrinydji's inheritance.

The opportunity to adopt non-Aborigines into the Yolngu realm in the 1700s or 1800s hardly existed. Most Macassans were merely classified by Yolngu as Yirritja, because this was the moiety of Birrinydji and all things associated with the new. In the latter years of the trepang trade, however, Macassans who were reported as having a basic understanding of Aboriginal culture and languages, were adopted into Yolngu clans. The last captain on the coast, Daeng Rangka, for example, was adopted by Ganimbirrngu as a member of the Warramiri clan. Legend has it that he took this adoption seriously. He had been a regular visitor to the coast for more than fifteen years and considered taking up his claim to membership by moving his home from Indonesia to Arnhem Land and accepting his role as broker, as part insider and part outsider. White settlement in northern Australia put an end to such ambitions, however, for Macassans were banished from the coast in 1907. Officials believed them to be a source of deadly diseases. There were also innumerable instances of mistreatment of Aborigines, and, furthermore, Macassans were making significant profits but not contributing taxes to the national coffers. In the early days of the Methodist mission at Galiwin'ku, male missionaries were also adopted into Yirritja clans, with their wives becoming members of Dhuwa clans. Galiwin'ku pioneer Harold Shepherdson was an adopted member of the Wangurri clan, and his wife was Djambarrpuyngu. By the 1960s, however, there were more than 100 non-Aboriginal mission staff, and each was developing close relationships with one or more Aboriginal families. It was no longer appropriate or desirable for intercultural relations to be bound by a moiety framework. Individuals were adopted on an individual basis and there were now just as many non-Aboriginal Dhuwa men as Yirritja women.

Yet well into the 1980s, if a senior member of the Australian government visited Elcho Island, it was the Yirritja people who would make the necessary arrangements, putting on welcoming dances, and so on. It was through them that the "adoption" process would take place. They would interact with whites in order to accomplish goals for the totality of Yolngu. This was also the case during Australia's bicentennial celebrations, when a Macassan prau, modeled on the seacraft of old, made a historic voyage to Arnhem Land to celebrate the ancient trade links between Australia and Indonesia. At this time, sword-wielding members of Yirritja moiety Warramiri and Gumatj clans, as well as the Dhuwa moiety children of Yirritja mothers, dressed in sarongs and performed Birrinydji dances as part of their greeting.

In 1988, however, a visit by the governor general to Galiwin'ku showed changes were afoot in the Yolngu political arena, just as there had been a metamorphosis in the way persons were adopted into the fold twenty years earlier. Yolngu of both moieties joined forces and presented the queen's representative with a bark painting of a picture of the crown and the Aboriginal flag and images from both halves of society—the crab (Dhuwa) and the crayfish (Yirritja). (See the photograph on p. 60) Only a few times previously had Yolngu come together to create a statement in art of their united stance on an issue. The first was the Adjustment Movement in Arnhem Land, which I discuss in the next chapter, and the other was the historic Bark Petition signed by Yirrkala Yolngu and sent to Canberra in an attempt to stop the destruction of sacred sites which would follow the construction of a bauxite mine on the nearby Gove Peninsula. Though the petition is on permanent display in Parliament House in Canberra, and the Adjustment Movement "memorial" is a treasured part of Australia's national estate, both initiatives were largely ignored by government. They remain, however, landmarks on the *Yolngu* political landscape.

Ten years later, a further shift had taken place. In 1998, the prime minister of Australia John Howard was welcomed at Galiwin'ku by Dhuwa moiety landowners, the Liyagawumirr, and their close

The 1988 presentation of a ceremonial bark to Australia's governor general.

affiliates, the Galpu and Gunbirrtji clans. This transformation in perspective from viewing the government visitors as Yirritja, with only one or two clans having the ritual authority to deal with them, to a situation in which the Dhuwa landowners have this responsibility prescribed under the Land Rights Act, marks a significant change. In examining this transition and its significance for reconciliation, the life story of David Burrumarra is of paramount importance. Burrumarra had been village chairperson for many years before the Dhuwa clans took responsibility for land management, and his ideas remain influential on a number of levels. This is because Yolngu political activity involving Balanda had long been viewed from one angle only: a traditional perspective involving the Dreaming figure Birrinydji.

The Warramiri have had a huge part to play in the way intercultural relations have developed in northeast Arnhem Land. In 1957, meditation upon the Birrinydji legacy by clan leaders who had an interest in Christianity led to a historic struggle known to the outside world as the Adjustment Movement in Arnhem Land. Orchestrated by the Yirritja moiety Wangurri and Warramiri leaders and initiated by David Burrumarra, decisions made at this time set Galiwin'ku on a course to reconciliation. By the 1980s Birrinydji was no longer seen to be of pan-Yolngu significance in this arena, as each clan had its own perspective on reconciliation, but the Warramiri continued to assert influence, as was their right by tradition. Burrumarra's last major public act was his Flag Treaty proposal, and both it and the Adjustment Movement are discussed next.

6

Warramiri Initiatives

Within the non-Aboriginal community, reconciliation means different things to different people. For some, reconciliation is a cause which involves the promotion of a wider-scale acceptance of the High Court decisions of Mabo and Wik: Aborigines are the prior custodians of the land; they have spiritual and historical ties to Australia that non-Aborigines do not share, but can appreciate, learn from, and aspire to. Others, claiming to speak for Aborigines, argue that reconciliation is extraneous to their needs, and that the day-to-day problems warrant far more attention and will not be solved by the signing of a treaty. There is also a faction of high profile spokespeople such as ex-Australian Prime Minister, John Gorton, who speaks of Aborigines as remnants from the stone age, and National Party leader Tim Fischer, who boasts of the physical and mental superiority of whites, pointing to the fact that even after 40,000 years, Aborigines still had not invented the "wheeled cart." In addition there is member of parliament Pauline Hanson who, in 1997, delighted in publishing the "facts" on Aboriginal cannibalism in her book *The Truth*,[20] as though this were pertinent in the debate over native title and reconciliation.

Given such open negativity, Aborigines realize that there are limitations on the extent to which adoption can be an avenue for the achievement of equality. The "sea of hands" sculpture gardens, growing all around Australia in support of reconciliation, hold out such a promise, but there is no consensus on what reconciliation means. Unrecognized in this broader political landscape are the specific ways in which the Yolngu are reconciling their own clan and moiety interests with the dominating Balanda culture. In this chapter, I trace developments in intercultural relations at Galiwin'ku over the past forty years from the point of view of Warramiri leader, David Burrumarra.

In Chapter 5, I described a transition from group to individual adoption of Balanda by Yolngu. In this chapter I suggest that this ideological shift was facilitated by the practice of Christianity and the

---

20. Hanson's source was the now-discredited anthropological writings of Daisy Bates.

legacy of membership-and-remembership or unity in diversity. An outcome of the Adjustment Movement, which I shall detail, was the ability to view major Wangarr or Dreaming figures as prophets of God. Each animating spirit from the sacred waterhole which gives rise to a unique human being is a product of God's will, as well as the totem. In other words, the new configuration transcended the moiety system. Christianity was relevant to the entire population. At this broader level of membership, Yolngu would look to the Balanda as both a group of fellow believers coming from a significantly different cultural background, and as individuals with no right to interfere with the Yolngu or their land.

Burrumarra's historical recollections, and the way he was able to adjust cosmology to past and present experience in his many projects, influenced the way northeast Arnhem Land Aborigines found a place for non-Aborigines in a "timeless" system emphasizing "changelessness in change" (see Rudder 1993). I begin the chapter with an overview of Burrumarra's life, and then examine his two major reconciliatory projects, Arnhem Land's Adjustment Movement and the Warramiri Flag Treaty proposal.

BURRUMARRA—A LIFE AT CENTER STAGE

While today every clan represented at Galiwin'ku has one or more *bunggawa* or "big men," from the 1950s to the 1980s there was one person only who would speak for the populace as a whole, and it was a member of the Yirritja moiety. In the 1950s it was the Wangurri leader Badangga. From the 1960s to the 1970s it was Badangga's Warramiri "brother" Burrumarra, and in the 1980s it was Badangga's and Burrumarra's adopted Wangurri son, George Daynumbu. In 1998 it was still a Yirritja person, Oscar Datjarangga, and he called Burrumarra "father." A member of the Gupapuyngu-Birrkili clan, Oscar acted as a representative of his Dhuwa moiety mother's clan, the Gunbirrtji, and also the Liyagawumirr clan.

In the 1950s through to the 1980s, Yirritja leaders governed in their own right. A number of Dhuwa clans, such as the Liyadhalingmirr and Djambarrpuyngu, considered Badangga to be their honorary head. A similar pattern was repeated throughout Arnhem Land as "big men" emerged to mediate relations between Aboriginal groups and between Aborigines and non-Aborigines. A tall stately figure, a diplomat and staunch advocate of Aboriginal rights, David Burrumarra was one of these prominent northern Australian Aborigines. He was a very influential man and considered himself, and was looked upon, as a person of consequence and authority among his people. He was a "big man" in a political sense and a "big man" for ceremonies, but as a Yirritja leader he was not a "big man" for Dhuwa sites and country in the vicinity of the mission.

There were many facets to the Warramiri leader's work at Galiwin'ku. Like other elders in the community, his daily routine involved the education of the young; the supervision of the "business" or ceremonial life of the clan—making arrangements for initiations and funerals; and the resolution of interclan disputes. Many of Burrumarra's generation agreed that three projects were of major concern. These were (1) to ensure the continued growth of an Aboriginal church led by an Aboriginal minister, (2) to see Aborigines managing fishing, mining, and tourism ventures on their land, and (3) to fight for a voice within the national political arena. Regarded by eastern Arnhem Landers as the father of sea rights, Burrumarra envisaged a time when there would be a partnership between Aborigines and non-Aborigines in the management of sea resources, reflecting the negotiation for the use of Aboriginal land by non-Aborigines in this part of the Northern Territory.

Burrumarra's contact with non-Aborigines included his work with missionaries, as teacher in the settlement school; with renowned beachcomber Fred Gray, as a trepang diver; with Australia's leading anthropologists, as a consultant; and with the government, as a spokesman for Aboriginal welfare and voting rights. He was also

Burrumarra holding a cycad seed grinding stone as a sign of ritual authority at a mortuary ceremony in the late 1970s.

involved in private enterprise. He put his hand to prospecting and in the late 1960s had small private pearling and typing businesses that were firsts for the community.

Burrumarra's contribution must be appreciated within the context of the changing nature of policies pertaining to Aborigines. Prior to 1967, Aborigines in the Northern Territory did not have the vote and had little control over who could enter their homelands. They had no power to direct the changes that were taking place all around them. Burrumarra saw his work with anthropologists and historians as being pertinent to his aims. As he said,

> My role has been to mediate between the people of Arnhemland and the newcomers, including missionary teachers, anthropologists and other scholars. While most Aboriginal cultures have faded out rapidly before the advance of European culture, my life's ambition is to see that knowledge of my own Warramiri and related cultures is preserved as far as possible. (Barnier 1978:205)

On the subject of belief, he said there were three principles he taught the young. He described them first in his own language then translated them into English.

1. *Nguwatjuma djama bunggul ga manikay Dholtji-wu ga nhunguway.* Participate in ritual life and perform the dance to the best of your ability. Do it for your homeland and for yourself.

2. *Marngi iya ngayiwu ga ngunguway.* Understand the land and everything on it so you can manage it properly.

3. *Marngi iya nhunguway djamawu ga bunggawayinyawu djinal Dholtji ga Australia-wu.* When you grow up and are a clan leader you will stand up and follow Aboriginal law not only for your homeland of Dholtji but for Australia as well.

"This is the real human rights," Burrumarra said.

An influential man with a very strong personality, Burrumarra often sparked debate in northeast Arnhem Land on the nuances of the relationship between Balanda and Yolngu. In a previous work (McIntosh 1992), I described him as a bricoleur or myth maker. The Adjustment Movement became the subject of anthropological texts and brought him international exposure. According to Kenhelm Burridge (1971), Burrumarra was the eccentric and charismatic figure that was so often associated with periods of rapid social change in so-called "cargo cults."

In his later years, many within the community of Galiwin'ku believed Burrumarra had too much power. He had been council chairman for twenty years although he was not a member of the landowning Mala. He also initiated and led a senior group which supervised the implementation of Aboriginal law in the settlement. His extraordinary knowledge of the Dreaming was unmatched and he was often accused of withholding from the younger generation vital information about the ceremonial life. In his critics' eyes, his receipt of an M.B.E.[21] in 1978 for his work in community development seemed to boost an already large ego. Some feared also that the award legitimated his status as the owner of lands well beyond his own Warramiri clan. Palmer and Brady (1983: 79) for instance assert:

> Burrumarra...claimed that if there was opposition to his [plans for development] he would call the Government, the Queen, the Navy...It was a brilliant move. He had sensed that the *Yolngu* were afraid of the world of European Australians. He however had successfully harnessed aspects of European Australian authority [through *Birrinydji*] for the furtherance of his own ends. He claimed he could provide protection for *Yolngu* if they complied with his wishes. He stated, "They feel safety because I'm in the midst. If I leave them, there is no shelter from the strong wind and rain."

Burrumarra said that the careful control of secret knowledge was the distinguishing mark of the landowner and Mala leader. But the world in which Burrumarra grew up seemed distant to the young and middle-aged men and women of Galiwin'ku in the 1980s. Burrumarra's knowledge came to lose its force and appeal. As far back as the 1960s, anthropologist Ronald Berndt wrote of how Burrumarra's attitude towards traditional knowledge and the way he advertised his advanced learning brought him nothing but ridicule. By 1987 Burrumarra was on the fringe of his own society.

It has been said that anthropological informants look for recognition in outsiders when it is not forthcoming in their own society. In Burrumarra's case this was not entirely true. The politics of the day centered on self-determination, which was equated locally with separate development, a reaction against assimilation and integration policies of the 1960s and 1970s. For Burrumarra the way this new policy was being implemented was contrary to the interests of Aborigines. "White" and "black" people had to live and work together and could share in the riches of the land and sea if all followed the laws of the country. The rapid changes of government policy toward Aborigines from one year to the next, the inconsistencies relating to mining and exploration on Aboriginal land, and the false hopes that a treaty would be enacted, all seemed to sabotage the achievement of Burrumarra's goals. With Aboriginal society and values perceived to be under threat on all sides, with the people torn between personal desires and the need to maintain the laws of old, Burrumarra claimed to

---

21. Member of the British Empire, an award.

be a guiding force for change. He did not want to see Yolngu left behind in the twentieth century. When asked why he had done the things he has done, he answered, "So we could be here in the future." After a long and controversial career, Burrumarra died on October 13, 1994, at the age of 77. In an obituary in *The Australian* (21 October 1994), his work in race relations was emphasized. In all his endeavors, the Warramiri leader sought respect and recognition for Aboriginal rights within a framework of national unity, and pushed for a reconcilement of interests in the early 1970s at a time when the Australian government was advocating a policy of assimilation or integration. Assimilation was the official policy of the Australian government towards Aborigines. The goal was that Aborigines, as Australian citizens, should follow the same laws, accept the same responsibilities, and live the same way as the non-Aboriginal majority. The vision of "sameness" promised by assimilation was never a viable option for Yolngu, and was rejected outright by Burrumarra.

SETTING THE SCENE

In the 1940s, the path towards achieving a rapprochement between Balanda and Yolngu was in the hands of Yirritja leaders, the followers of Birrinydji. It was very different from today, as at that time, Aborigines were wards of the state and had little or no power outside of the traditional arena, and even this was under threat from mission teachings. There were few visiting dignitaries, contact with the outside being only the anthropologists who came to study the Yolngu, the missionaries who came to save the Yolngu, and the developers who wanted to make money by mining Yolngu land. Paternalism was the central feature of relations between non-Aboriginal authorities and mission inmates, and Northern Territory Welfare Director, Harry Giese, was a "protector" in an old-fashioned sense. As Burrumarra said, "In those days, we were told what to do." There was little opportunity for widescale adoption of Balanda as a means of asserting authority in the non-Aboriginal world. No bridges link island Galiwin'ku with the mainland; the only ships that made this a port of call were mission luggers, and passenger entry was restricted. Even now, on the adjacent mainland, there are no jetties, merely cuttings in the mangrove forests from where a boat can berth or be launched. Telephones arrived only in the 1980s, as did television and video. A mission radio-phone was not accessible to the general public, only to senior Aborigines with personal or business needs preapproved by the missionary.

However, even then Yolngu were affirming their sovereignty in accordance with their traditions. They spoke for the country, for the rocky peninsulas and islands, for the tidal creeks, coral reefs, and open sea. They were "one" with the fish, the birds, the animals of the plains. Only Yolngu sang for the emu, the kangaroo, the marlin, and only Yolngu had personal names that tie their spirit to the eagle, the bamboo, or to the eucalyptus tree.

THE ADJUSTMENT MOVEMENT IN ARNHEM LAND

The Adjustment Movement was undoubtedly one of the most significant and controversial events in recent northeast Arnhem Land history. It involved the display of formerly concealed sacred emblems representing all Yolngu in northeast Arnhem Land (see the photograph below). Men erected their revered totem poles and then sat back, Burrumarra said. No public statement was made to the missionaries or government, though in Berndt's (1962) account, he labeled it a form of "adjustment": clan leaders were presenting a case for the retention of traditional values while attempting to adapt to the inevitable changes introduced by white Australians. For senior Yolngu, the action was an affirmation of the Aboriginal presence and a proclamation of sovereignty. The official policy of the day may have been *terra nullius*, but Aborigines were intent on making themselves visible to the outside world. No longer would Elcho Island Yolngu keep all their laws secret.

Elcho Island's Adjustment Movement memorial.

Burrumarra had his own ideas about what an adjustment would entail. He sought an end to the "promise" system of marriage and wished to introduce monogamy in accordance with missionary teachings, but there was too much opposition from older men (Shepherdson 1981:23). Burrumarra also tried to set up negotiations with the government for improved community services and the recognition of Aboriginal rights. There were also claims for compensation. Aborigines had been forced into a situation of making profane that which was sacred, but according to Maddock (1972:2) Burrumarra was "deluded or misguided" in thinking he would succeed. The community of Galiwin'ku was remote and just one of many Aboriginal settlements across the "Top End" of the Northern Territory. As the ex–Elcho Island missionary Harold Shepherdson says, the effects of the movement were primarily restricted to northeast Arnhem Land (personal communication 1990).

The outside world was encroaching on the Yolngu from all sides, and the decision to display crucial religious icons in a prominent area in the community had an extraordinary impact. Many women and children ran away from the settlement, for in the past, they would be killed for setting eyes upon these totem poles. But male leaders reassured the community that a monument or memorial had been erected to a way of life that was changing beyond all recognition. Revealing the *rangga* was a way of letting non-Aborigines know that the Yolngu possessed title deeds to country.

The public showing of sacred objects irrevocably altered their character for future generations, and there were mixed feelings amongst the population. As Burrumarra said, "We felt good about it. Good, but sorry. We knew things would never be the same again." The Warramiri revealed a whale *rangga* linked to Birrinydji, the Wangurri, a mangrove worm design associated with Lany'tjun, the Liyagawumirr a goanna symbolic of Djang'kawu, and the Madarrpa a *rangga* for the sun, and so on. Not all the *madayin* were revealed however, a point which various commentators use as evidence that Aborigines were, at least in part, leaving their options open.

The Adjustment Movement represented a thorough break with the past, and anthropologist Ronald Berndt identified the initial stirring for the movement with Burrumarra, who was then forty years of age. It was Burrumarra who convinced the more established Aboriginal leaders at Elcho Island to join the movement and reveal their *madayin*. Berndt says Burrumarra had

> ...for some time been thinking...about the problem of adjusting or bringing together traditional Aboriginal and introduced ways in order to achieve the maximum benefit from the latter.... On the one hand he wanted change from the outside with greater rapidity. On the other...he did not want them to overwhelm his own society and culture.... If this

loss of identity were to be avoided then some re-orientation of traditional life would be necessary. (Berndt 1962:39)

Events had come to a head, Berndt (1962:39) said, after the visits of the American-Australian Expedition to Arnhem Land in 1948 led by C. P. Mountford and of Dr. Richard Waterman and his wife to Yirrkala in 1952. Berndt quotes Burrumarra as saying,

[Anthropologists] take photographs of [our] sacred things and show them to all the people throughout Australia and other places.... We're not supposed to show these [*madayin*] ...to just anybody.... [We] saw a film at the Elcho Church. It was from the American-Australian Expedition and it showed the sacred ceremonies and emblems. And everybody saw it.... We've got no power to hide [these *madayin*]; they are taking away our possessions. Are we to lose all this? Our most precious possessions, our [*madayin*]! We have nothing else; this is really our only wealth. (Berndt 1962:40)

Some scholars suggested that the movement was something akin to a Melanesian-style cargo cult, for Yolngu, in return for showing their most precious belongings, expected great riches (e.g., Borsboom 1992:16–17; Burridge 1971:172; Kolig 1989). But such categorization is offensive to Yolngu, for while there was an expectation of some form of material compensation as a result of the changes that were being forced upon Aboriginal people, there was also an agenda of "composition." There was a hope that relations between Yolngu groups, for the first time living together as a single community, would be consolidated, as would relations between Aborigines and the wider community. Prior to the Adjustment Movement, Burrumarra said, all the clans had their own ideas about right and wrong. As Cawte (1993:16) adds, there was widespread feuding which jeopardized the growing community. Living in accordance with the rules laid down by missionaries and also the laws of non-Aboriginal Australia, was itself a reconciliatory act, but it was also a necessary step for a community that wished to have access to the amenities of a similarly-sized non-Aboriginal township.

While the Adjustment Movement is now viewed in terms of key individuals, that is, Yirritja leaders Burrumarra of the Warramiri clan and Badangga of the Wangurri clan, and Dhuwa leaders Walalipa and Mayamaya of the Golumala and Djambarrpuyngu clans, at the time it was perceived to be under the leadership of a man that Burrumarra described as his professor. Berndt (1962:41) explained that the people were "lifting up" the Yirritja "big man" Badangga to lead all community groups, presumably in line with an image of Yolngu as followers of one God. There was a conscious attempt at redefining social organization. The Yolngu were to be a single unified block of clans and Christianity was put forward as legitimizing the unity of Dhuwa and

Yirritja moieties. As a cooperative group, the Yolngu would be in a stronger position to voice their demands vis-à-vis the Welfare Department, missionaries, and developers. Christianity was being presented as a belief that transcended all others, but it was not at the expense of clan beliefs. The founding ancestors of the Dhuwa and Yirritja moieties, Lany'tjun and Djang'kawu had been redesignated as Old Testament–type prophets. This is the process of membership-and-remembership that I describe in detail in the next chapter. Aborigines would become members of a broader community by accepting new rules, but they would also remember their origins.

A striking sculpture by Badangga in the memorial highlights this ideology. It was based on Lany'tjun, the All-Being associated with the Yirritja moiety, and it had a cross built on top of it. Of its significance, Berndt wrote (1962:60),

> The Christian cross…at the apex of the [*madayin*] is "Badangga's believing." In his own words, "helped" by Burrumarra, [he said] "Before, [Badangga] was leaning on the old laws. But in 1956 he changed himself and he also changed genesis [the *Wangarr or Dreaming*] to follow Christian fellowship. He kept this *madayin*, but the Bible is there too. He would like to keep both laws. [He] has combined both ways, so that he can put all of his children in school to become missionaries."

Yet it was only a matter of years after the memorial was erected that mining operations commenced in Gove, largely ignoring the rights and wishes of Aborigines. It was as if the Adjustment Movement had come to nothing, and sunk without a trace. This is how many of the residents of Yirrkala view the movement. A political split between Galiwin'ku and Yirrkala originates here. While Elcho Islanders stressed belief in Christianity and the revealing of *rangga* as an avenue to reconciliation, at Yirrkala, Yolngu pursued a different strategy. They began a protest movement which led eventually to the proclamation of the Aboriginal Land Rights Act. Much of the "memorial" has now decomposed and faded from view, and with it has gone the memory of Yirrkala's involvement.

At Galiwin'ku, Yolngu lived in sight of the memorial and were continually reminded of their commitment to change. Each and every clan at Galiwin'ku highlights the role played by their antecedents. I could stress the innovative ways that Dhuwa clans such as the Golumala, in particular the descendants of Walalipa, have achieved a monopoly on managerial positions within the community. To one extended family belong the store manager, the school principal, the senior health worker, the church minister and member of Australia's Aboriginal Reconciliation Council. I could also place the spotlight on the Wangurri descendants of Badangga, the Adjustment Movement figurehead, and their achievements. Badangga wanted his children to follow two laws: the Bible and the Dreaming (*Wangarr*). His children included Wes Lanhupuy, the first Aboriginal member of parliament in the Northern Territory; George Dayngumbu, once council chairperson and also head of the Aboriginal Benefits Trust, and Timothy Buthimang, who has established gardens on homelands throughout northeast Arnhem Land.

However my focus is on the Warramiri and the role of the Adjustment Movement agitator and his descendants. There is Burrumarra's eldest son Andrew Leku, a Minister in the Uniting Church at Milingimbi who has worked in Aboriginal communities throughout Arnhem Land; Terry Yumbulul, an internationally known artist who has exhibited his traditional designs in New York, Paris, and London; Mungutu, a federal government public servant in Melbourne, more than 3,000 kilometers away. Burrumarra also has three daughters, Rrapu, Mulwanany, and Lambu. All live at Galiwin'ku and are active members of the church. Rrapu is married to the senior traditional landowner of the settlement area, a match arranged by Burrumarra.

In the remainder of this chapter I examine Burrumarra's last public act towards reconciliation, the Flag Treaty proposal, and in later chapters discuss how the legacy of his work is relevant in a whole range of contemporary reconciliatory developments at Elcho Island.

FLAG TREATY PROPOSAL

While Burrumarra's influence declined in his later years, his clan continued to support him. In 1989 Burrumarra and his two brothers, Liwukang and Wulanybuma, created a large flag painting as the basis for deliberation on the need for a treaty between Aborigines and non-Aborigines in Australia (see the photograph on page 72). They were seeking to plot a course toward the future for all Yolngu, to direct their thoughts and actions along specific paths to reconciliation.

Private meetings were held with Mala leaders from all over north-east Arnhem Land during which Burrumarra revealed his design and explained its significance. Some of the images had never been openly displayed before and the Warramiri action provoked much debate at Galiwin'ku and in neighboring communities. In many ways it was a repeat of the Adjustment Movement.

Through a color leaflet distributed to Aboriginal organizations and government bodies (see Burrumarra n.d.), the Warramiri leaders made a public call for Aborigines Australia-wide to construct a series of new national flags incorporating sacred symbols which would unite black and white people under the laws of the land and sea, as in the Warramiri painting. The theory was that in the future there would be not one but many Australian flags, each containing Aboriginal symbols relevant to the area in which it was flying, depending

The Warramiri flag depicting Birrinydji, the octopus, as well as the Union Jack.

on its meaning to the inhabitants. For instance, if one were in Sydney, the flag might incorporate images of the rainbow serpent and dolphin or other designs, reflecting the law or *Rom* in that area. The common factor with all the Australian flags would be that the "sacred" symbol of Great Britain, the Union Jack, would appear in the upper left-hand corner, as in the current Australian flag. The uniting of the symbols in a common design would be symbolic of a wider coming together, Burrumarra suggested. Respective histories would be united, and people could share in the riches of the country as equals.

Burrumarra's views often received exposure in the national media. In a press release dated 15 December 1989, he said,

> Aborigines own the continent of Australia.... Some two hundred years ago strangers declared war on the Aboriginal owners and the strangers won, but the land did not recognize it...
>
> Aborigines and the newcomers are still strangers to each other. I am a stranger to white law and the land has always seen "Europeans"...as outsiders. But the war between black and white is nearly over. We are just about in a position to use both of our eyes to look at each other. In the past, it has always been with one eye—looking at each other sideways with much suspicion. Why can't we live together on equal terms?...
>
> The Federal Government has talked about a treaty or compact without any real commitment.... I feel...that to recognize each and every aspect of the country by the laws by which it exists is much more than a treaty between people. It

is a show of respect to the land. [The Warramiri Treaty proposal] is a step towards a time when white and black can all live with pride in their community and their country.

In the proposal, Warramiri flags would fly only in Warramiri territories, but they would be recognized Australia-wide, as an archetype or "starter." They would be the prototype from which all other flags would evolve. In Burrumarra's eyes, their flag was to be the "big one." Thus in a united Australia, the position of the Warramiri would presumably be paramount. Yet, the treaty proposal was not only a case of one group attempting to elevate its status over and above others (though there is no doubt that Burrumarra wished to see his intellectual prowess and the legacy of his clan acknowledged). The Warramiri proposal had as its central aim a desire to reformulate the way Aborigines and non-Aborigines relate to one another and Burrumarra viewed his flag as the logical outcome of a particular way of understanding the history of contacts with non-Aborigines. The younger generation of Warramiri refer to it as a traditional outlook, or "the way of the old people." Fundamental to this view is Warramiri ownership of a body of *Rom* associated with the ancestral being Birrinydji, depicted and revealed to the public for the first time in the treaty proposal. The law of Birrinydji is a legacy of contact with Macassans, and through it, the Warramiri leaders believed they had a mandate for mediation with non-Aborigines.

THE ABORIGINAL AND THE YOLNGU FLAGS

Harold Thomas, an Aborigine from Brisbane, designed the official Aboriginal flag that flies throughout Aboriginal Australia. Divided horizontally into two halves, there is a circle in the middle. The colors red, black, and yellow symbolize the red earth of the outback and the Aboriginal blood spilled upon it, the black skin of the indigenous inhabitants, and the yellow sun. It is flown by Aboriginal organizations; people wear shirts and hats with the design upon it, and in many places it flies alongside the current Australian flag. At Galiwin'ku, the Aboriginal flag adorns the council chambers, where it symbolizes the struggle of all Aborigines for the recognition of their native title rights. The Warramiri flag, in contrast, stresses both resistance to non-Aboriginal hegemony, and accommodation of outside influences.

In Australia throughout the past ten years, there has been a major push to change the national flag, coinciding with a desire to see Australia become a republic by the year 2001.[22] The Warramiri proposal

---

22. Economic events have slowed the momentum for change.

was only indirectly linked to this. In a press release going back to 1979, Burrumarra declared:

The Whitlam era saw a raising of the Aboriginal people to a level previously unknown. There was an expectation that the Aboriginal people would achieve a status that existed in pre-white days, when [we] were masters of [our] own destiny. Since [the Whitlam years] the status of the Aboriginal people has gone down. Certainly the money is still forthcoming, but it is giving without listening. There is no sense of partnership, no real respect for the Aboriginal law and feelings.... We believe that all things dealing with mining, fishing, forestry or other occupations, which effect the Aboriginal people, should be discussed between *Balanda* and *Yolngu.* This is the proper way to do things for Australia...

We Aborigines call ourselves citizens of Australia since assimilation in 1962[23] when we signed ourselves into the book of Australia. Yet we are not fully connected with the important things. Our standard should be in Parliament House where the law is made; in the law courts where it is carried out, and in the hospitals where the miracles of healing are done. In all these places we should be equal. (McIntosh 1994:115)

In his biography (McIntosh 1994), Burrumarra spoke of the Warramiri Treaty proposal as being the culmination of the Adjustment Movement in Arnhem Land, in which the memorial reminded Yolngu of their past and of how they had set their sights on a future to be shared with non-Aborigines. His public statements on the relevance of Birrinydji in the reconciliation process were, however, cryptic. Apart from the distribution of the color brochure and several other press releases, information about the treaty proposal has been limited, principally because we are dealing with subject matter of significance at a number of levels:

1. Flags are *rangga* associated with Birrinydji and a related Dreaming entity Walitha'walitha.

2. In the sacred Birrinydji narrative, Warramiri Yolngu once possessed the wealth of the other (both Macassans and Europeans), but through misadventure, this was lost.

3. Birrinydji first contact narratives point to a need to reevaluate the relationship between Aborigines and non-Aborigines.

---

23. Some Aborigines in the Northern Territory received the vote in 1962, five years before the 1967 referendum which finally recognized Aborigines as Australian citizens.

4. Prior to the treaty proposal, the narratives were considered secret and overly obscure and not to be shared with non-Aborigines.

Birrinydji is shown in the Warramiri design as the foundation of the Union Jack. This was deliberate. The Union Jack is "all the same" as Birrinydji's flag, Burrumarra ventured. Defying any possibility of a simple explanation, he said it represents "the same idea" but with one major difference. Birrinydji is for the Yolngu. "The Union Jack symbolizes the taking of the land, and ignoring Aboriginal rights." There is a desire, however, to "bring the Union Jack on side."

Burrumarra's worldly influence and his ability to reconcile cosmology and contact history has placed the Birrinydji narrative at the forefront of the reconciliation debate in northeast Arnhem Land. The unfortunate contemporary living conditions of Aborigines in Arnhem Land and the complex nature of relationships with non-Aborigines ensure the continued relevance of this Dreaming. Burrumarra, for example, saw a need for new laws that would confirm the respective rights of Aborigines and non-Aborigines. He remarked to the author:

> *Birrinydji* in the past dictated that we must honor him and follow his law. In the new world we…[must] live together not apart. This is why [our homeland] is still important in today's world, just as before…
>
> Today, people live as one group. "Black" can marry "white" and vice versa. This is part of the lesson of the Treaty. We are different today than before. We live by a new law. Our histories have merged. The law of the past was [*Balanda* for *Balanda*] and *Yolngu* or *Yolngu*. This is *Birrinydji's* law.… But we can share the future if there is equality.… We ask [the Governor General], Can we be equal in your eyes?

Beyond the confines of northeast Arnhem Land, the impact of the Warramiri flag treaty proposal has been limited. In Sydney in 1996, various Aboriginal organizations assembled flags representing a number of clan groups for the historic Rocks district (or first settlement area), but the accompanying public statement made no reference to Burrumarra or the Warramiri. At Elcho Island and Yirrkala, a number of clans, both Dhuwa and Yirritja, created their own versions of the Warramiri flag, though none contained the Union Jack. The Gumatj-Burarrwanga flag, for instance, contained the image of the Bible, an anchor, and two swords—all Birrinydji symbols. Such treaty-inspired flags, however, were not put to use in the cause of reconciliation. Within the community of Elcho Island they emerge during school graduations or at funerals, where they signify and celebrate the clan of the graduating student or of the deceased.

THE NEW GENERATION

A new generation of Elcho Islanders continued where Burrumarra's work ended. The sons and daughters of Burrumarra, Liwukang, and Wulanybuma are heavily involved in church affairs, local community politics, the sea-rights campaign, and the homelands movement. The younger generation has had far greater exposure to the non-Aboriginal world than the Warramiri elders ever had, and they have their own strategies for achieving a rapprochement with Balanda. For example, in the 1970s, there was a movement by Galiwin'ku Christians to evangelize the nation—to bring Christianity back to the "whiteman." As detailed in Chapter 8, Christian groups in Arnhem Land see respect for the law of the Bible as a way to bring about reconciliation in Australia because all people are equal in God's eyes.

In elaborating on the ways in which Warramiri Yolngu are striving towards reconciliation, it is necessary to introduce the reader to traditional Warramiri perspectives on the past, some of which openly conflict with the findings of historians. So in the next Chapter I examine the pervasiveness of ideas on reconciliation through Birrinydji in the Yolngu domain, both in the Dhuwa and Yirritja moieties.

7

Reconciliation and the Dreaming

A perverse dualism appears to characterize non-Aboriginal views of Aboriginality. On the one hand, Aborigines are noble savages and are seen to embody the creative formative power of the original sense of the sacred (Lattas 1997:247). Yet on the other hand, projected onto them is the view that they are ignoble and treacherous, the "missing link" connecting humanity to a violent animality from which it has evolved (ibid:251). Perhaps as a consequence, non-Aborigines perceive the Dreaming in diverse ways. American author Marlo Morgan's (1994) book *Mutant Message Down Under,* about the "real people," was a huge international success despite the fact it was fictitious. The author romanticizes Aboriginality and posits a situation in which all people in the world are mutant offshoots of the "real people," the Aborigines, and mutant technology is destroying the planet. In order to save the world, we must learn from the Aborigines. Alternatively, for many non-Aborigines in Australian society, Aboriginal beliefs are considered to be readily fabricated and, by appealing to the guilt of the nation, can be successfully harnessed to block development. In fact, an indigenous person who proffers information about a sacred site these days is almost certain to be branded a fraud, a money-hungry schemer, or not a genuine Aborigine. Birrinydji confronts this duality. Emerging in the latter stages of the Macassan era, the Birrinydji narrative challenges non-Aboriginal ideas of sovereignty and focuses attention on the history of race relations.

In this chapter, following a brief overview of the relevance and meaning of the Dreaming in contemporary Aboriginal life, I ask the questions, What were the unforseen consequences of the adoption of whites into the Yirritja moiety? What is the significance for the Warramiri of aligning themselves with a Dreaming being in the image of a white man? I examine contemporary accounts of Birrinydji and the associated story of Walitha'walitha with the aim of highlighting the main features of the Warramiri approach to reconciliation. In a theme developed in the remainder of the text, I suggest that the

Warramiri strategy is based on (1) opposition to the encroachment of non-Aborigines, (2) accommodation of non-Aborigines by acknowledging common spiritual interests, and (3) seeking compromise solutions which support local power structures and allow Yolngu to benefit materially from contact.

LIVING THE DREAM

Aborigines are constantly reminded of the legacy of the creation period because everywhere that Dreaming beings went, they left behind something of themselves. The octopus, cuttlefish, and hawksbill turtle are emblems of ancestral beings who created the islands that are traditional Warramiri homelands. The changing of the tide is indicative of the movement of the ancestral whale being. Similarly, the swordfish, the fish with sails like a boat, and the bird with a tail like a metal ax are a legacy of Birrinydji and signify to the Warramiri the continuing relevance of his laws. Aboriginal religion combines such belief in the supernatural with the practical concerns of daily survival. Who hunts, who gathers, where one can go, and who has the knowledge necessary to make such decisions are either laid down as law or can be interpreted from Dreaming narratives.

Sacred sites are reservoirs of supernatural power, and it is this power which ensures the country's renewal though it is not automatic. Traditional ritual practice ensures that humans are able to access this divine power, but it is only available at certain times and places, and then only to the right people (Berndt 1962). In a sacred ceremony, for instance, Aboriginal leaders recreate events from the Dreaming in a way reminiscent of how they were first experienced. The symbol of a deity (in the case to be examined in this chapter, Birrinydji's mast and flag) is positioned on ritual ground so as to attract and hold the spiritual force of the Dreaming, while actors play out the parts of the drama accompanied by the sounds of the *didjeridu* (drone pipe), *bilma* (clapsticks), and a *manikay* (song). When the ritual conditions are satisfied, the deity may bestow its power or meaning to participants through the leader. In the days of Macassan trepanging, the Birrinydji ritual would be performed upon receipt of trade goods from the visitors. According to Burrumarra, the gift acknowledged that Balanda and Yolngu shared a common life force through Birrinydji.

Dreaming tracks or songlines cover more than the territory of a single clan, and each group is responsible for maintaining their part of the law. All Mala in northeast Arnhem Land, for example, own a specific aspect or interpretation of the moiety narrative, and the operation of the moiety depends on all the clans working in harmony. As I describe later, in the case of Birrinydji, responsibility for the performance of ritual was shared among three Yirritja moiety clans but from a Warramiri perspective responsibility also spread beyond the confines of the Australian mainland to seafaring groups from the islands of eastern Indonesia. In traditional Aboriginal society, religion and politics were inextricably intertwined. However, as a result of contact with outsiders—Macassans and especially Europeans—nonrational modes of thought now play much less of a role in the political process. Since the advent of the mission at Galiwin'ku, the Aboriginal *Weltanschauung* has been subjected to a process of rationalization, and a new generation of Warramiri have been forced to rethink many of their traditional concepts. According to Kolig (1989), drawing on the experience of Aborigines in the Kimberley region of Western Australia, the meaning of myth and ritual is drastically changing. In some cases, the Dreaming no longer provides the eternal, immutable blueprint for the world and human existence. Too much has changed. Some Aborigines do not believe, for example, that in performing a rite they will achieve a particular outcome. A significant number of Aborigines today try to shape their political destiny in the Australian nation primarily through their involvement in the wider political process. They participate in bodies established by non-Aborigines, such as local councils, land councils, and housing societies; and vote in local, state, and federal elections, and for representative Aboriginal bodies such as ATSIC They are also aware of the benefits of using the media to create a sympathetic response in the wider public.

The Dreaming, for many, has become a reservoir of political symbolism but not instrumentality. Fertility ritual, for instance, rather than being a precondition for species survival, expresses an entitlement to land in the face of non-Aboriginal encroachment (Kolig 1989). Aborigines need to remind themselves, as well as others, of their privileged position in relation to "country."

The history of race relations in Arnhem Land has been such that many Yolngu feel great resentment towards Balanda, and the Birrinydji ritual provides an avenue for the expression of negative feelings. Dhalwangu and Gumatj clan members treasure their detailed knowledge of Birrinydji's songs and ceremonies and carefully maintain sites in the landscape, but they are not able or willing to speak about the related narrative. The Birrinydji Dreaming has become all but a mythless rite. The Warramiri, however, being advocates of a reconciliation with Balanda, have elaborate stories concerning Birrinydji, but even they are cautious about revealing them. Whites might come to believe that the Dreaming condones their discriminatory practices. What follows in this chapter is an account of a traditional perspective on reconciliation, emphasizing Birrinydji, from the viewpoint of the Warramiri and, in particular, David Burrumarra and his descendants at Galiwin'ku.

A "New" Traditional Perspective on Birrinydji and Walitha'walitha

All that is known of the Birrinydji Dreaming has been passed down to the present through many hands and interpretive processes. The Warramiri leader Bukulatjpi is credited with "doing the thinking" and uncovering the "truth" about Birrinydji and the Macassans. In many parts of Australia the first settlers were deemed to be ancestors returned from the dead, their light skin color being evidence of the bodily decay that takes place in the weeks following a death. Bukulatjpi, living on remote Cape Wilberforce in the mid-1800s, understood that Macassans were not Yolngu or in any way divine. Rather, their inordinate material wealth and willingness to share this with Aborigines in exchange for labor was having a major impact on Warramiri lifeways. Possession of modern technology was equated with the visitors being recipients of Birrinydji's inheritance. Bukulatjpi reasoned that something had gone wrong at the beginning of time for Birrinydji was an Aboriginal Dreaming and its inheritance was the right of clans such as the Warramiri, so long as his ritual was performed. But it was the Macassans that performed his dances on the beaches of Arnhem Land. Yolngu had long "forgotten" them.

Just as a totem represents the outward form of a Dreaming being, a Macassan *bunggawa* (boat captain) by the name of Luki appears to provide a visual image of what Birrinydji is like. Otherwise, Birrinydji is indistinguishable from other Dreaming figures. Sacred *rangga* that represent his legacy are the basis of extensive clan alliances within the Yirritja moiety. Numerous totemic species owe their form to his intervention and Birrinydji is associated with specific tracts of country belonging to the Warramiri, Dhalwangu, and Gumatj clans, just as with Lany'tjun.

Bukulatjpi viewed Birrinydji as a Dreaming figure that controlled the seasonal movement of the Macassan trading fleet and also the winds that would bring the visitors to the coast each November. Birrinydji provided these fishermen with skills to fashion swords from coastal haematite outcrops and pottery from local antbed, and to grow rice and plant other foods in Warramiri *billabongs* or waterholes. But Birrinydji did not act alone. Bukulatjpi understood that he was answerable to a higher Dreaming authority—*Walitha'walitha*,[24] or Allah.

Birrinydji and his wife Bayini were ancestors of Yirritja Yolngu— creational figures that emerged from the Australian mainland at a point beyond memory. Birrinydji ordained that certain non-Aborigines would come to Arnhem Land to make the land and the people strong

---

24. From the Islamic chant—La ilaha illa'llah: "There is no god but God."

and bring them up to date. First there were mysterious black whale hunters from the mythical islands of Badu to the northeast of Galiwin'ku; then mythical golden-brown workers for Birrinydji, known also by the term *Bayini;* then historical light-brown Macassans from the northwest; and finally white Japanese pearlers in the 1920s and European colonists. The color change in the visitors in this constructed history from black to white corresponds with a change in attitude towards reciprocity in dealings with Aborigines, and therefore knowledge or ignorance of Birrinydji's law.

Aborigines and whale hunters were united in Walitha'walitha through the whale, an outside symbol for Birrinydji. Together they upheld the law of the sea. The alliance between the two was such that the souls of the Aboriginal dead from the Yirritja moiety went on the backs of whales to the land of the dead, guided by these hunters. The Bayini, on the other hand, after introducing the laws of Birrinydji to the Yolngu, kept the secrets of iron-making and weaving to themselves when they departed. Certain Macassan leaders recognized the law of Birrinydji and respected Aboriginal sovereignty, but most did not and there was great disparity in wealth between visitors and landowners. Finally, Japanese and Europeans totally ignored Aboriginal rights and there was no reciprocity in the relationships.

By far the most significant of the "waves" of contact was with the mythical golden-skinned Bayini, the bringers of Birrinydji's laws to Aborigines. The Warramiri homeland of Dholtji became a center for iron manufacture, boat building, and rice, clothing, and pottery production. According to Burrumarra, when Aborigines and the Bayini were united, they prospered. But over time relations soured. Warramiri Aborigines desired only good, but "bad came too" Burrumarra said. A "fire came to the Yolngu" and "there was great bitterness between white and black." The spirit of the dead or Wurramu took over Yolngu lives. Birrinydji wanted to bring more non-Aboriginal people to Arnhem Land but Walitha'walitha sent Birrinydji and the newcomers away, for Walitha'walitha could see how the Yolngu were suffering. So the Bayini left before their work of teaching was completed. Their parting words to the Aborigines, "From now on you must look after yourself," was the signal for the beginning of an era of impoverishment for Aborigines. The maintenance of the status quo required ceremonial input from blacks and whites, but as Burrumarra said, "Birrinydji did not want to stay in Australia, but he left the Wurramu and Walitha'walitha here." Birrinydji and Bayini's legacy is the continuing unpleasant consequences of contact, and ideas of the good life and salvation in Allah.

The Yolngu did not cope well with the new world that Birrinydji had offered up to them, for *yatjkurr,* or "unholy" ideas, had ruled their past behavior, or so they came to believe. This is one interpretation that the Warramiri posit as the reason for joining the mission at

Galiwin'ku in the 1940s. They looked to Balanda missionaries for another chance at life in the new world. Promised was a return to the days when Dholtji was a regional capital and Yolngu enjoyed the wealth of whites. All that the Aborigines had to do was follow church law. But it soon became apparent that European and Tongan missionaries had little to share with Aborigines except ideas of a paradise to come in the after-life. According to the Warramiri elders, it was a fundamental miscarriage of justice that the Balanda had the proceeds of Birrinydji and yet were completely ignorant of his law.[25]

In the early years of the century, the Warramiri had aspirations that members of their clan would acquire mobility, talent, and worldly status as followers of Birrinydji. This Dreaming represented the wealth that comes from the earth, Aboriginal earth, assets to which non-Aborigines alone appear to have access. In telling the story of Birrinydji in the 1980s, Burrumarra wanted the world to come to understand that in matters pertaining to the land and sea, "Aborigines are the law in Australia." Birrinydji may be a Dreaming in the image of the Other, and Walitha'walitha may be the God of the Macassans, but they are also Aboriginal Dreamings.

THE MAST AND FLAG

Yolngu remind themselves of the ancient nature of belief in Birrinydji and Walitha'walitha by pointing out how widespread are items of material culture and terminology associated with these Dreamings. On remote beaches and isolated headlands, in the middle of bustling settlements, in cemeteries or at places were a Birrinydji ceremony has been held, one may find a tall bamboo pole with a strip of cloth attached. In the major communities of northeast Arnhem Land one encounters a variation on this theme—a replica of a ship's mast—a flagpole—complete with elaborately decorated flags. Both refer to Bir-

---

25. This constructed past can be seen from another angle. In the Dhuwa moiety is the Djang'kawu narrative, which is relevant to the entire Yolngu population, for the mother of a Yirritja Yolngu is always Dhuwa. At one level, it deals with the loss of power of women to men at the "beginning of time." Women alone once safeguarded the sacred *rangga* and performed the necessary rites to "uphold the universe," but one day, the *rangga* were stolen by men. From that point onwards, women had to look away when men performed the sacred *Ngaarra* ceremony, for they did it so well. In Burrumarra's (and Bukulatjpi's) narrative, Aborigines were once powerful, but now "whites" keep that power to themselves. But just as men cannot exist without women, non-Aborigines need Aborigines. Their wealth and influence comes from Aboriginal land and an Aboriginal Dreaming, just as a man's body, his *rumbal* or truth, comes from the woman.

rinydji and Walitha'walitha. The bamboo pole is associated with funerary rites, and at the cemetery at Galiwin'ku there are perhaps a hundred in various stages of dilapidation. The mast is usually located on graves of Warramiri, Dhalwangu, or Gumatj clan leaders, but more commonly at places where influential indigenous leaders sat to deliberate the politics of the day. The ship's mast stands at least three meters high and is painted with distinctive black, white, yellow, and red triangles, associating it with the Yirritja moiety. At Galiwin'ku, the Warramiri mast is located where Nyambi, Burrumarra's older brother, used to live. Apart from the fact that it has an attached plaque with an inscribed Christian message, there is no hint of a link between the presence of the mast, Aboriginal belief in God, or the reconciliation process.

It was Burrumarra's task in the later years of his life to convince non-Aborigines that Yolngu have a specific role to play in "holding up the universe" for all Australians. One method employed was his Flag Treaty proposal, and for inspiration he drew upon the meaning of the Warramiri ship's mast *rangga*.

In discussing intercultural relations, Yolngu will often inquire about the level at which one wishes to speak. There is the "government line" where one speaks of party politics and the structure and functioning of Aboriginal organizations; there is the "church line," where talk will center on the progress being made by the congregation to bring Christianity back to the whites, and banish the practice of sorcery and cursing; and there is the "Yolngu line," where the topic is the Dreaming and politics. In most cases people will only discuss matters pertaining to their own clan, and discourse is characterized by discussion of matters of an "outside" public or historical nature, as opposed to subjects from the sacred or secret "inside."

Warramiri attitudes on reconciliation are embedded in "inside" and "outside" Dreaming narratives associated with first contact and the ship's mast. Although it is not possible to say that in the past there was a widespread uniformity of belief in Birrinydji in northeast Arnhem Land, there is evidence to suggest that in the 1920s first contact and colonization was contemplated by members of both Dhuwa and Yirritja moieties in terms of this Dreaming, as I will detail.

Aboriginal oral historical accounts describe how the Macassan prayer-man would climb the mast and chant for Allah—the most High God—prior to the journey home to Indonesia (Berndt and Berndt 1954:45–46). Earlier records indicate that when a mast of a Macassan boat had broken or a man was about to die, a ceremony involving the mast would be performed. It is implied by anthropologists that Aborigines adopted this ceremony as their own and, in the process, attached additional meanings to its performance relevant only to themselves. In the 1920s, for instance, anthropologist Lloyd Warner (1969:420), witnessed the way in which Warramiri and Gumatj clan members would pick up a dead body during a funeral and move it up and down as if they were lifting the mast, while others danced as if pulling on the rigging in order to raise the sails. (Today Yolngu lift the coffin in a similar fashion.) They would then sing for Allah or Walitha'walitha, describing the song as a Macassar prayer, and ask for unspecified blessings from this "man-god in the moon." Warner chronicled how the mast ceremony facilitated the passage of the soul of a deceased Yirritja Aborigine to an unknown land of plenty to the north. The soul was to sail away just as the Macassar prau used to do.

All Yolngu have some memory of Macassans through stories passed down from generation to generation, but it was only Burrumarra, according to his brothers, who could speak the truth as it was known from the "inside." Even men in their seventies deferred to Burrumarra's interpretations. This was because the Warramiri are the primary custodians of Birrinydji, and, according to tradition, Birrinydji speaks to Yolngu through the leader of the clan.

Warramiri oral history details the gift in 1907 of a mast and flag to the Warramiri leader Ganimbirrngu by Daeng Rangka, the last trepanger to visit the Arnhem Land coast. For Yolngu this was interpreted as the reenactment of a Dreaming incident in which the ancestral entity Birrinydji planted his flag at Dholtji at the beginning of time. Daeng Rangka's mast was to replace an old decaying mast at the Warramiri homeland, which itself was a replica of a large metal pole which had stood on that same site in Birrinydji's day. Described as being like a chimney associated with iron smelting, the mast stands for Birrinydji's law or the new world order imposed on Aborigines following first contact—an order that "turned the Aboriginal world upside down" (Burrumarra personal communication 1988).

Statements by Yolngu elders such as "the mast and flag is the way the law is carried," suggests that the mast was placed on Arnhem Land shores in a way reminiscent of the English hoisting the Union Jack in 1788, but it is not straightforward. Throughout the colonized world there are examples of the ritual significance of the mast and flag separate from that assigned by colonial powers. In East Timor, the mast and flag represented the lost brotherhood of Timorese blacks and European whites. The return of the young brother in the form of the colonial Portuguese was a mixed blessing. The newcomers held sway in politics, symbolized by the flag, but the old brother that stayed behind, the Timorese, asserted that they forever would be senior partners in matters pertaining to the mast, or land (see Traube 1988). In New Zealand, Maori leader Hone Heke repeatedly cut down the mast of the English governor, for its presence threatened Maori ideas of sovereignty. Hone Heke would rather wage an all-out war against the settlers than allow the colonizers' flagpole and standard on his land (see Sahlins 1985).

The Arnhem Land situation has much in common with the East Timor case study. Burrumarra said that Macassans visiting Arnhem Land shores recognized the old mast and flag at Dholtji, which had then been in Warramiri possession for countless generations, and knew that Aborigines were the custodians of a law that had once united them at some point in the distant past. Aborigines and the people of Sulawesi were one through Walitha'walitha, just as Christianity was now seen to unite Yolngu and Balanda.

When anthropologists Lloyd Warner and the Berndts encountered Birrinydji ceremonies in the first half of this century, they witnessed, in the bodily movements of performers, a powerful demonstration of Aboriginal authority as owners of land. Aborigines recreate the planting of the mast and the assertion of Birrinydji's dominion over the land, they swirl Birrinydji's swords overhead, and quick-step as if propelling Birrinydji's boat. As Burrumarra argued, the purpose of the ceremony is to "show the Yolngu," that is, to make it apparent that the Yolngu have an important ceremonial role to play in maintaining a law from which ostensibly whites also draw their power.

In the 1940s the Berndts recorded 150 *garma* or "outside" songs pertaining to Macassan influences. By the late 1980s, however, these same songs were regarded as "inside" or sacred. Yolngu at Galiwin'ku were now openly practicing Christianity, and there were conflicts between the two beliefs. Statements of Yolngu leaders, such as "The followers of Birrinydji should be Christians," or "We are Murrnginy, we believe in God," or "Walitha'walitha is one and the same as the Christian God," are indicative of the transformation taking place. From the 1950s, Burrumarra said, there was a conscious effort to restrict and change what was known of the Aboriginal past. The old ways were "too hard, too far, and too difficult to explain" to the younger generation. The view of Yirritja moiety Aboriginal leaders was that there was great similarity between Walitha'walitha and the Christian God, and there was a possibility of confusion, so they openly promoted the latter and hid the former. Birrinydji, however, could not so easily be set aside. Birrinydji rituals are the joint possession of a number of clan groups, including non-Aborigines, the Yolngu believed.

By 1988, the Birrinydji theme was being used explicitly as a rallying point for pan-Aboriginal resistance to non-Aboriginal incursions. Birrinydji's influence was now seen to encompass all places affected by European colonialism. Former "Australian of the Year," Gumatj spokesperson, and lead singer of the rock group *Yothu Yindi*, Mandawuy Yunupingu used Birrinydji dances in songs about maintaining one's Yolngu identity while "living in the mainstream"; Terry Yumbulul of the Warramiri clan stirred Yolngu to unite and demand their rights by invoking the memory of Birrinydji; and Burrumarra used the image of Birrinydji on a flag he wished to see flying from Parliament House in Canberra, as a symbol of Aboriginal reconciliation. The place of Birrinydji in today's world is ambiguous and changing, and the reemergence of this law in the 1980s after almost disappearing in mission times is evidence of a tension that exists between timeless ideals and inconstant social realities. In the 1950s, Burrumarra believed that the establishment of the Christian mission at Galiwin'ku was Birrinydji's plan for Yolngu. They would become Christians and Birrinydji could "put down his swords" (McIntosh 1996). In other words, there would be peace and harmony as Aborigines reaped the benefits of the Dreaming. This was not to be, of course, and in the 1980s Burrumarra reevaluated his strategy and decided to make public many of the myths of Birrinydji as part of his reconciliation proposal to the federal government.

MEMBERSHIP AND REMEMBERSHIP

Following the Adjustment Movement in Arnhem Land, all Dreamings were repositioned in a broader universe—a universe that included non-Aboriginal Australians. Walitha'walitha was spoken of as an angel of the Christian God, and Birrinydji became an equivalent term for the Aboriginal struggle. This repositioning is membership-and-remembership. In a vision of the world united by Jesus, for instance, each social unit within the whole represents a self-governing entity. Through Christianity, Yolngu and Balanda are united in a larger system of belief which sees all Australians as being members of a single family. While Walitha'walitha and Christian beliefs are interpreted in relation to one another, their significance for Yolngu is seen separately, at different levels of membership, that is, Christianity is for all people, Walitha'walitha is for Macassans and Yolngu, Birrinydji is for the Yirritja moiety, the whale is a Warramiri totem, and so on.

But membership-and-remembership is more than this. It refers to the interplay of "inside" and "outside" and mythical and historical narratives. Yolngu may be dominated by non-Aborigines as a consequence of history, but they "remember" Walitha'walitha. They may be united with non-Aborigines through a belief in God, but they "remember" that Birrinydji is an Aboriginal Dreaming and that the wealth of non-Aborigines comes from Aboriginal land.

There is no word in Yolngu *matha* that translates as membership-and-remembership, but it is an ideology that is basic to the Yolngu belief system, as noted in Chapters 1 and 2. Burrumarra was the first to coin the expression, but I have heard many other Yolngu use variations of it. Dayngumbu of the Wangurri clan, for instance, often refers to "familyship" in discussing the "remembership" inherent in moiety organization. Each Mala in the Yirritja half of Aboriginal society shares the one ceremony, and it is performed at regular intervals as a show of solidarity. Yet the Dreaming being Lany'tjun also gave to each group certain other bodies of law relevant to their unique histories. Warramiri Dreamings are centered on the sea. Ritharngu Dreamings are centered on the dry inland stretches. Yet at a moiety level of membership, a Dreaming being in the form of a duck called *Muthali* acts on behalf of Lany'tjun when it travels from the inland to the sea to build its nest. Muthali is credited with giving shape to the Warramiri islands by the power of the flapping of its wings and also of introducing to the Warramiri the system of kinship fundamental to moiety operation. So the Muthali is a moiety signifier, but it is also symbolic of the association, at a clan level, of the Warramiri and Ritharngu.

Profound intercultural lessons concerning membership-and-remembership also arose as a result of Aboriginal contact with the Macassans. A few words of Macassan origin drawn from personal names of Warramiri and Gumatj Yolngu and the Birrinydji theme highlight this legacy.

- *Rraya* is a name that refers to "taking up where someone else left off." The English beachcomber Fred Gray carried out trepanging at a site that Macassans had worked, in a practice inaugurated by the Bayini. This is *Rraya*. Yolngu draw on this word as evidence of how Dreaming beings established the world and its rhythms, providing models for human action.

- *Gupaniny* is a site in Warramiri territory where Bayini carried out iron-making, cloth production and boat building. Yolngu go to this place today and remember their past. According to Burrumarra, Yolngu ask themselves: Were the Bayini right or wrong in taking their trade secrets with them when they departed from Arnhem Land? Is this why Aborigines have so little and non-Aborigines so much?

- A further word drawn from the Birrinydji theme that inspires membership and remembership is *Rrandhing*, the anchor of Birrinydji's boat. This term refers to a behavioral standard. When the anchor is in place, "no wind or rain will move the boat from its mooring." In a similar way, the anchor is seen to hold the Warramiri people in place. They will never run or be driven away from their land by non-Aborigines.

Jewish theologian Martin Buber (1949) proposes a similar outlook to membership-and-remembership in his essay "In the Midst of Crisis." He describes a community as a circle with a clearly defined center. Members have a common relation to this center which overrides all other relations. The community, that is, the circle, is described by the radii and not by the points along its circumference. The common center must be something concrete, like a sacred text such as the

Torah, a person (like Jesus Christ), or a set of rituals (as in Confucianism). As people see, study, and come to understand the center, they become aware of the divine, and their attention is turned outward to the world around them, to larger levels of membership, where their work lies, for it is beyond this circle or community that the authority and authenticity of the center is proven.

In northeast Arnhem Land, Yolngu look to the Dreaming as the sacred center of their community, and, in a perspective based on membership-and-remembership, they consider their emerging roles and responsibilities in a world lying well beyond their homelands. In a similar way, non-Aborigines who are striving to build a future together with indigenous people see at the center of the sacred circle the land which gives inspiration and pleasure, and from which their livelihood is made. For Yolngu, the achievement of reconciliation will be a testimony to the truth and continuing relevance of the Dreaming. For non-Aborigines, reconciliation aims to promote a much desired sense of belonging in the knowledge that white Australia has a black history.

Birrinydji and Reconciliation

For many Yolngu, the fact that Birrinydji takes the form of a white man is evidence of membership-and-remembership. His symbol, the mast and flag, signals "remembership" of long ago, of the perceived partnership between Aborigines and non-Aborigines, and also Aboriginal "membership" in belief in this law. The mast itself represents the earthly dimension, the place of struggles between "black" and "white." The flag on the other hand, in Burrumarra's words, represents the heavenly dimension and the idea that all people are, or will be, united. A legacy of contact between Aborigines and Macassans and spoken of with honor, the ship's mast stands for Birrinydji's law, which Macassans, Japanese, and Europeans ignored or "forgot." The mast gives physical form to, and is a reminder of, an eternal quest by Yolngu for prosperity and deliverance. Following Burrumarra's lead, lessons from the "inside" and "outside" pertaining to the mast permeate discussions about human rights and the treaty.

When Birrinydji left the country, with him went the affluence that only non-Aborigines possess. Aborigines have the songs and the stories of Birrinydji, sites in the landscape, and a memory of a grand and noble past. In Burrumarra's words, the Yolngu have "plenty but nothing." Because of Birrinydji, the earth is a place of struggle, and Dreaming narratives inspire followers of the law to pursue the earthly paradise to come. The mast and flag therefore speak to a deeply held belief by the Warramiri that non-Aborigines can never totally dominate Aborigines because white and black people are united (members) in a belief in God. In Burrumarra's view, if there is to be reconciliation in Australia, non-Aborigines must acknowledge (or remember) that their power and influence over Aborigines comes from an Aboriginal Dreaming. Alternatively, there needs to be recognition of the privileged place of Aborigines in relation to land and an equitable sharing of the proceeds of development.

8

Christianity and Self-Determination

If reconciliation entails the adoption of non-Aborigines by Aborigines, and of Aborigines by non-Aborigines, in ways which affirm their mutual worth, then the insensitive methods employed in implementing a policy of self-determination in the 1970s were not in the interests of reconciliation. In this chapter I examine the changes taking place at Galiwin'ku at this time and address the direct correlation between the implementation of self-determination and the rising popularity of Christianity.

IMPLEMENTING MARGINALIZATION

As a response to the 1967 constitutional referendum, self-determination emerged as a federal government plan for dealing with Aborigines, replacing earlier ideas of assimilation and, in Queensland, integration. Aboriginal organizations would deliver services to their own people in appropriate ways, developing enterprises through which communities could become economically independent. Based on anti-racist ideas, the discourse of self-determination promised an end to the racial hierarchy established by the colonial state. However in attempting to reshape communities, there was little or no recognition of the specificities of Aboriginal culture. In fact, the manner of enforcement only served to perpetuate Aboriginal dependency. While economic independence was equated with the reinvigoration of culture, Aboriginal views were ignored in the quest for rational and effective business management (Cowlishaw 1998). Aboriginal communities became dependent on the skills and services of a new clique of managers promising future autonomy, so long as *their* decision-making role was not questioned. As Cowlishaw (1998) declares, the practices of state officials became a "glass barrier" precluding Aborigines from responding either as expected or as they themselves desired.

Aborigines were expected to be jubilant, for political autonomy would render them independent of local "whites." Indeed, the policy was welcomed at Galiwin'ku, but in a few short years it became obvious that instead of moving closer to autonomy, Yolngu were moving further away from it. The departure of missionaries led to the ruination of the community gardens and the collapse of the local fishing industry. Aboriginal council workers were jailed for embezzlement of community funds, and contracts for housing projects worth hundreds of thousands of dollars were paid out without completion of the work. Yolngu were continually judged as wanting in their ability to manage the community. As Cowlishaw (1998:150) discovered:

> what was not recognized was that the unprecedented plans could only be realized when fundamental changes took place in the Aboriginal clients.... Certain kinds of subjects had to be produced who would take part in the procedures which the state demanded.

According to the ARDS report, Yolngu in all spheres of employment were unprepared for self-management. For instance, in the 1970s, there was an initiative by Health Department officials for the Aboriginalization of health centers throughout the Northern Territory. In places such as Milingimbi, Umbakumba, and Pularumpi, non-Aboriginal staff were being phased out as Aborigines took on responsibility for local health care. At Galiwin'ku, health workers resisted this move. They had basic medical training and were comfortable with their role as co-managers of the health center with mission staff. Whites and blacks had their own specific areas of expertise. Aborigines would manage routine procedures, community relations, and public health education, and would work hand in hand with non-Aborigines, who tended to more serious ailments and administrative tasks. But with the deteriorating health of the Aboriginal population in the 1980s, Elcho Islanders were deemed to be unsuitable recipients of state funding. Soon there were more white staff than ever, and Aboriginal health workers at Galiwin'ku, formerly confident in their position as respected community workers, were now marginalized as the increasing ill-health of the population was blamed on their inexperience and lack of education.

This pattern was to repeat itself throughout the community. Without the cooperation and support of mission staff, Aborigines found the settlement difficult to manage. Residents watched helplessly as the expansive community gardens fell into ruin, school attendance dropped by half, and health problems reached crisis proportions. The beautiful coconut trees which lined the streets were cut down; garbage was no longer collected; and the streets became lined with empty tins, plastic bags, and disposable nappies. A report in the national magazine *The Bulletin* in 1988 described Galiwin'ku as the filthiest village in the world (Jarrat 1988). A place once believed to be paradise by the older generation was now bordering on a disaster area. Petrol sniffing became rife among teenagers and alcohol and kava were consumed in ever-increasing quantities. The people were ineffective managers of their own lives, let alone their community. More and more non-Aborigines arrived at Galiwin'ku to address the situation and by the late-1980s, a majority of the roles of responsibility in the community were held by Balanda. Meetings would be held between Aborigines and the newcomers, but these were only for officials to get authorization to run a project the way they wanted to, in a manner considered rational and cost effective (Cowlishaw 1998). Aborigines were squeezed out of positions that they formerly held, and while many began to undertake intensive training courses, others pursued an entirely separate course.

The sacred ceremony associated with the rainbow serpent, the *Gunapipi,* once banned from Elcho Island by missionaries and clan leaders because it promoted promiscuity, was suddenly in vogue. Sorcery was rife in the community and the Liyagawumirr landowners of Galiwin'ku, disturbed by these developments, threatened to curse the entire settlement and send everyone back to their own homelands. Yet they too delivered their young and irresponsible youths into the hands of Gunapipi ritual leaders in the hope that the intense discipline surrounding the year-long ceremony would reorientate them to traditional ways.

Mirroring the rise in visibility of the sacred Gunapipi ceremony was a movement which denounced both sorcery and the beliefs associated with the rainbow serpent as the work of the devil. It was the locally-led and powerful Aboriginal movement known as the Black Crusade, whose purpose was to bring Christianity back to the white man (personal communication Djinyini Gondarra 1986). Belief in Jesus was to be the means by which Yolngu could pursue an Australian Aboriginal identity and control the effects of the increased power and involvement of non-Aboriginal agencies in Aboriginal lives. In other words, Elcho Islanders wanted to be able to regulate their relations with whites in self-enhancing ways. Christianity promised relations between Balanda and Yolngu of a spiritual order, not on the degrading level of Aboriginal inefficiency, illiteracy, or incompetence in the white world.

THE ARDS REPORT

The 1994 ARDS report was entitled "Cross-Cultural Awareness Education for Aboriginal People," and was submitted to the Northern Territory Office of Aboriginal Development by the Aboriginal Resource and Development Service. The work was produced by Uniting Church employees with long experience in northeast Arnhem Land and close personal ties with the Aboriginal communities. The consultation process, conducted over six months in 1994, sparked great interest and attracted considerable local Aboriginal support. The report's objective was to examine ways to address the unfortunate state of affairs at Galiwin'ku and the nearby community of Ramingining. It pulled no punches. In the study, a picture was presented of Yolngu as being totally mystified by white law and unable to function within structures established by non-Aborigines. Mystification was a term coined by renowned sociologist and educator Paulo Freire (1973) to describe the state in which a group of people are bewildered and trapped in dependency and overwhelmed with feelings of inferiority and powerlessness.

For many Yolngu the report was a breakthrough. On the one hand it was the first major attempt by Balanda authorities to come to an understanding of Yolngu concerns. On the other, there was a perception that the secret knowledge or magic that underlay Balanda success was to be revealed to them. Using the terminology of Paulo Freire, the report labels the idea of "secret knowledge" as characteristic of situations in which people find themselves to be completely dominated by others because events and forces shaping their lives are not understood intellectually. People are fatalistic and dependent on those in authority. According to Freire, they conform to the image of themselves superimposed by the other culture. In these circumstances, Yolngu feel inferior, unintelligent, and are perceived as being followers of a way of life that Balanda perceive as illegitimate. The ARDS report investigated ways of confronting this state of intellectual marginalism. The solution proposed was the institution of a series of training programs which would explain the functioning of the Balanda world by using Yolngu concepts and understandings. The purpose was the reorganization of community structures so as to integrate local ideas and traditional ways of thinking. The question of the link between Christianity and the quest for self-determination was left unresolved. There was no discussion, for instance, of the connection between the growth of the Aboriginal church at Galiwin'ku since the 1970s and the increase in the non-Aboriginal presence and the expansion of debilitating social problems.

CHRISTIANITY AT GALIWIN'KU

In 1974, in accordance with changing policies in Aboriginal Affairs, the Methodist Overseas Mission had withdrawn from the Elcho Island community, and Aborigines took over the administration of settlement and church affairs.[26] The process of reconciling traditional Aboriginal beliefs and practices with Biblical teachings then accelerated, though it is still a subject of community discussion. Minister Dr. Djiniyini Gondarra, for instance, advocates a need to maintain traditions whereas Minister Mawunydjil Garrawirritja disagrees, viewing a complete

---

26. In 1978, the Methodist Church became a part of the Uniting Church of Australia.

break from the past as a necessary step forward for the Yolngu so that in the future all people will be united in Christ. One Aboriginal lay preacher argues that it was the decision of her father and grandfather that her family follow a particular "line." These were people who had an intimate knowledge of the Dreaming, and they made a new law for all to follow. Another lay preacher believes the word of God has released the Yolngu from a "dark and brutal past," and he views Christianity in terms of social justice. He says that it is only by following this path that inequalities between Aborigines and non-Aborigines will be alleviated. Still others consider Christ to be a manifestation of certain Aboriginal mythological beings, for instance Walitha'walitha. Despite this split in the way Yolngu understand the relationship between their own cultural inheritance and Christianity, there is an overall agreement that Elcho Islanders follow the one God. This is membership-and-remembership. Another point of agreement is that by following the Christian God, Yolngu do not become Balanda. The practice of Christianity is not equated with being assimilated into the non-Aboriginal world. Burrumarra exclaimed in one meeting of church elders that Aborigines needed to keep their culture strong and argued that only by stressing differences between white and black could Aborigines maintain their status as spokespersons for their homelands.

CONFRONTING MARGINALIZATION

Aboriginal identity at Elcho Island is framed in part in terms of belief in the Christian God, but Christianity is also a structure for the

Elcho Island men honor the pioneering missionary Harold Shepherdson in front of the Galiwin'ku community church in 1992.

expression of ideas on what the nature of the relationship between Aborigines and non-Aborigines should be. That it has provided an avenue for confronting the intellectual marginalization that came in the wake of the mission experience is evident in developments over the past twenty years, in particular the Galiwin'ku evangelical movement known as the Revival, and the Warramiri Ngaarra ceremony, to which members of the church and government were invited to participate.

The Elcho Island Christian Revival

A landmark event in the reconciliation of beliefs at Elcho Island was the Christian Revival of 1978, when, as anthropologist John Rudder (1993:72) suggests, the Holy Spirit came to Galiwin'ku. This was a time of prophesies and visions. In one documented case, an Aboriginal fisherman named Djamila was diving in the waters around Elcho Island when he found a rock at the bottom of the sea in the shape of Australia, in fulfillment of a prophesy by the Wangurri clan leader Buthimang. This rock was evidence of a time to come when all the peoples of Australia would be united in Christ and in that future the position of Aborigines would be paramount.

The Revival is commemorated each year in a weekend of celebrations in March with hundreds of visitors arriving from all over the country. Prior to 1978, despite the Adjustment Movement, only a small percentage of community members were baptized Christians (Rudder 1993:53). Leading up to and following the Revival, however, prayer meetings became a regular nightly occurrence involving the majority of island residents. In many ways the 1978 event at Elcho Island was viewed as the "Second" Revival, a repeat of the Adjustment Movement (Rudder 1993:73–74). It was the sons and daughters of the major figures of the 1957 movement that were now promoting belief in Christianity. Wuyatiwuy and Rrurambu, sons of Wangurri leader Badangga and Djiniyini Gondarra, the son of Golumala leader Walalipa, were its leaders, along with Liyagawumirr elders Djilipa and Bunbatju.

In the wake of the Revival, some Elcho Island Christian leaders saw themselves as possessing a mandate to bring Christianity to the rest of Australia. Known outside of Arnhem Land as the Black Crusade, Aboriginal groups from Galiwin'ku traveled thousands of miles throughout the Outback spreading the "Good News" (Bos 1988). I was present at a Christian festival in Alice Springs in central Australia in 1991, for instance, when an Aboriginal elder praised the efforts of visiting Elcho Islanders for transforming his homeland in the Outback from an Old Testament "valley of dry bones" into a living community. He said that when the Elcho Island evangelist Rrurambu and the Black Crusade came to his settlement there was not a single living thing there. All the people were spiritually dead, but then they found "a new way" and life returned to the valley. These same people had been members of a church mission for some time, but what was important was the fact that Aborigines brought the word of God to them. When Rrurambu read from the Bible, everyone listened.

The growing trend on Elcho Island at this time was for Jesus to replace the major Yolngu ancestral beings, Djang'kawu and Lany'tjun, as the foundation of the Aboriginal way of life. However, there was far from universal agreement on this development. While sympathetic, Burrumarra stood by the original Adjustment Movement position in which both traditional Aboriginal beliefs and Christianity would be held side by side. Neither would have precedence (personal communication 1990). The Revival doctrine was for Christianity to be the one and only law in the community and there was little public discussion on the important ways in which older beliefs were still relevant in people's lives, even though it appears to have been a concern for many.

Despite attempts by some Yolngu to downplay it, a largely unspoken concern in the community is that Christianity actually did pose a threat to identity. Buthimang, the Wangurri and Christian leader, said that he feared that in the future there would only be one clan at Elcho Island, the Christian clan. Membership-and-remembership was foundering as an ideology. Laws at family, clan, and moiety levels determine links to country, intergroup relations, and marriage procedures, and this was imperiled if one law dominated all others. Looming in the minds of the Yolngu is the threat of chaos that would accompany the loss of authority by leaders. So, while the alignment of Christianity with Aboriginal traditions in the Revival was supported by Burrumarra, he continued to support the Adjustment Movement position of laws overlapping and entwining in important ways but with neither having precedence—only different audiences.

The Wangurri/Warramiri Ngaarra Ceremony

One of the most influential events in achieving the reconciliation of Christianity with the legacy of Arnhem Land ancestral beings, at least from the perspective of certain Wangurri and Warramiri leaders, came with the performance of a Ngaarra at Elcho Island in December 1993. This ceremony has been well documented in the literature (e.g., Keen 1994; Warner 1969). The Warramiri/Wangurri variation deals with the founding actions of the moiety ancestral being Lany'tjun and his emissaries. It is described by Yolngu as being about the history of the world and one's place in it.

While other clans had held their Ngaarra ceremonies, the Wangurri and Warramiri had not staged their version since before the time of the Adjustment Movement, with Burrumarra emphasizing that even though the ceremony remained of the utmost significance, he was worried that it was no longer relevant to the way the Yolngu were now living. The Wangurri leader, Dayngumbu, for instance, was a "born again" Christian, desiring a clean break from the past. Buthimang however believed the ancestral being Lany'tjun to have been an emissary of Jesus, and when he delivered Christian sermons, he often wore the sacred *madayin* associated with this Yirritja moiety ancestor. Still other Wangurri leaders had different ideas. Warramiri clan leaders, likewise, were largely divided in terms of residence and belief. Liwukang and Wulanybuma of the Warramiri clan, for example, saw *madayin* as the Yolngu Bible whereas Burrumarra saw a place for both beliefs in the Yolngu way of life.

Burrumarra declared that it would be pointless to hold a Ngaarra ceremony if the real power in people's lives, that is, the government and Christianity, were not represented. It would be nothing more than a mockery of sacred traditions (McIntosh 1994:xvii). Younger leaders, however, were starting to complain that they did not know what to tell the young about the past or how to explain the relationship between various Yolngu groups. There was concern that no policy had been agreed to by all on the reconciliation of the "old" and the "new."

In late 1993 a compromise was reached and the ceremony commenced. A cross was positioned in the sacred ceremonial ground, just as a cross had been placed on one of Lany'tjun's *madayin* in the Adjustment Movement. At the end of Lany'tjun's dances each day, the performers would bow their heads in prayer. While the Ngaarra is said to be about Lany'tjun "holding the country" on behalf of the Yolngu, the new addition was Lany'tjun "praying to God for the people" (Dayngumbu personal communication 1993). As in the Adjustment Movement, the message for Warramiri and Wangurri clan members was that no longer could there be any mention of the heritage of Lany'tjun without reference to Christianity. Yolngu were first and foremost Christians, but their identity as Aborigines was inextricably linked to their clan and family history. The Wangurri clan went so far as to baptize their land in a ceremony in 1996 in order to affirm membership-and-remembership.

ABORIGINAL SELF-DETERMINATION

Elcho Islanders openly resent the fact that they have made virtually no impact on the Balanda world, whereas they have been compelled to make substantial changes in their way of life to accommodate Balanda. Their response over the past forty years has been to forge an identity that is quintessentially Yolngu but which embraces and attempts to manage the Balanda world. In the 1950s the momentum of change involved the release of sacred, secret information in the Adjustment Movement as a means of affirming Aboriginal interests in "country," and there was an expectation that people would be compensated by non-Aborigines for revealing their most treasured possessions. From the 1970s to the 1990s, we see accelerated efforts by Yolngu at determining the nature and intercultural significance of their belief in the Christian God and also considerable local support for training programs designed to educate Aboriginal people in the ways of the Balanda world. Yolngu want access to that "secret knowledge" long denied them by missionaries and government workers which has kept the Balanda rich and Elcho Islanders poor all these years. As an ideology, membership-and-remembership suggests not an end to white involvement in community affairs, but having non-Aborigines work with Yolngu as partners.

In the following three chapters, I describe the preconditions for Aboriginal adoption into the non-Aboriginal world. For Yolngu, these preconditions are the recognition of sea rights, equitable dealings with development companies, and a voice on the international stage as a sovereign power in their own right.

9

Aboriginal Management of the Sea

There are many aspects to Warramiri involvement in the reconciliation cause, and one of the most important is the fight for the recognition of Aboriginal sea rights. In October 1994, Yolngu at Galiwin'ku held a press conference and made a televised call for an indigenous marine protection strategy for Northern Territory coastal waters north to the Australian–Indonesian boundary. In this zone, said the Yolngu, were sacred Aboriginal totems, song cycles, ceremonies, and the pathways of creational beings. The aim of the call was to initiate discussion on the need to combine both Aboriginal and non-Aboriginal knowledge in the management of the Arafura Sea, which the Yolngu call *Manbuynga ga Rulyapa,* and for Aboriginal people to progressively reassume responsibility for various levels of management of the area, based on their customary laws.

Critics of the Yolngu joint management plan suggest that Aboriginal interests in the seas could not extend further than the horizon when viewed from the highest point of land. Flimsy bark canoes and, with the arrival of Macassans, dug-out sailing canoes were inadequate for open-sea travel. Yet many Yolngu elders possess detailed knowledge of sacred sites over 100 kilometers to the north of Arnhem Land. From a Dreaming-inspired perspective, rights to these sites stem from the creative exploits of the ancestral octopus and whale and draw upon the memory of contact with Badu Islanders, the first "wave" of foreign contact in Arnhem Land.

The chapter begins with a discussion of Aboriginal marine interests with an overview of Warramiri sea beliefs and Burrumarra's views on the significance of the wave of contact associated with whale hunters. I then analyze the proposed Indigenous Marine Protection Strategy. Here, as in the ensuing chapters, I examine (1) the response of Aborigines to perceived illegal activities (resistance), (2) shared beliefs with the other (accommodation), and (3) the path to reconciliation. The voice of a new generation speaks out on sea rights in this chapter. Sea degradation and overfishing in the Arafura basin is a twentieth-century phenomenon, and Yolngu leaders, inspired by contemplating the Dreaming, bring to the negotiating table a solution for the long-term protection of northern Australian waters.

WARRAMIRI SEA DREAMINGS

Aboriginal knowledge of the sea is all-encompassing, based as it is on the accumulated wisdom of thousands of generations. All living things found in the sea and named have their place in ritual life. Yolngu personal names refer to sea themes and feature in songs which make reference to the flow of rain and spring water down to the sea, tidal action upon reefs and beaches, or the uncovering of resource-rich mud flats. Burrumarra, as a name, refers to the skeleton of a Yirritja stingray, while the Warramiri leader's other personal names, Wurrthunbuy and Djumidjumi, also have a sea focus, reflecting Warramiri origins. The former, for instance, is a coral reef to the north of Elcho Island associated with the Dreaming entities *Ngulwardo* and *Marryalyan*, and the latter is a Macassan word for the squid. Burrumarra's sons are named for the octopus (*Manda*) and the whale Dreaming (*Yumbulul*), while his brother Wulanybuma's name means "open-sea swimmer."

The moiety founder, Lany'tjun, is associated with totems from the land and the coastal fringe, but the Warramiri heritage centers on the sea. The law there stems from the creational being Ngulwardo, the old man or king of the sea. Ngulwardo, the seafloor bedrock and coral reef, communicates directly with Warramiri Yolngu as they travel by canoe or swim in deep water, or indirectly through an intermediary, the totemic being Marryalyan. This being works in a "laboratory," to use Burrumarra's terminology, under the reef, transforming itself into various Yirritja species such as the *Limin* (squid), *Mardi* (crayfish), *Nyunyul* (cuttlefish), and *Manda* (octopus). Marryalyan is also the force which drives the seasons, initiating and terminating the wet and dry seasons that dominate the climate in north Australia.

The whale is the highest of Warramiri totems. Though it is Yirritja and connected to Lany'tjun, and its bones are "made" of coral and therefore a legacy of Ngulwardo, the whale is its own Dreaming entity. It is a product of the seawater itself and is most closely associated with Birrinydji, for its spout represents the steam issuing from an iron furnace within its belly. In many narratives, the whale is also synonymous with the whale hunter's sailing canoe.

The beaching of a whale is a blessing for the land, Burrumarra said. Warramiri Yolngu would converge upon it, perform sacred ceremonies in its honor, drink oil from its head, and rub their bodies with its grease and blood. In the Ngaarra ceremony, Warramiri mimic the copulation of whales because whales are the foundation of Warramiri existence. Just as Gumatj Yolngu "grew up" or settled where the ancestral crocodile laid its eggs, or Ritharrngu Yolngu where the emu made its nest, the Warramiri found residence at those places where the totemic whale beached itself at the beginning of time. The influence of the whale extends well beyond the Australian coastline, far out to sea. In fact, the Warramiri believe in a link to all peoples and places associated with the whale's travels.

WHALE HUNTERS AND THE WARRAMIRI

Historical records confirm that Sama-Bajau (sea gypsies or whale hunters) accompanied Macassan trepangers on their voyages to Arnhem Land, but in Warramiri songs they represent the first wave of foreign contact to Elcho Island.

Whale hunter Dreaming narratives can also be viewed in other ways. For example, visitors can be viewed as Yolngu returned from the dead; as variations on a story line associated with the seasonal availability of marine resources; or as part of Yirritja creation narratives linked to various sites in the totemic landscape. The abundance of narratives in the Warramiri repertoire suggests extensive contact. There are legends of a hunting party from what is now Indonesia being towed onto the Arnhem Land coast by a harpooned whale; of dark-skinned people mysteriously arriving on the coast and either being frightened off, or living peaceably with Yolngu; and of ceremonies held together on Elcho Island beaches.

Yolngu refer to the whale hunters as their brothers. They were black in skin color and, apart from having boats, knives, and tobacco, were seen to have a similar level of technology and understanding of the world. In fact, Burrumarra was of the opinion that the first visitors were more "on the law" of the sea than Aborigines, and he referred to these "pre-Macassan" voyagers by the Bahasa Indonesian title of *bunggawa* (or leader).

Perhaps the most important legacy of contact with whale hunters is the narrative in which the whale hunters kill their prey and ritually divide it up, giving the tail to Yolngu, while keeping the upper body and head for themselves. The whale's tail is a symbol of Yirritja moiety unity and is shared between the Warramiri, Mildjingi, Lamamirri, Gumatj, and Munyuku clans. When Yolngu see the whale swimming in the open sea, they are reminded not only of a law that binds clans in the moiety, but also their age-old partnership with non-Aborigines. The whale's tail design is used by various artists in sacred Yirritja artwork, though in a cross-cultural sense it is also important. In the

Barunga Treaty painting, jointly produced by Aborigines Australia-wide as a demonstration of solidarity in their quest for reconciliation, the north-east Arnhem Land component took the form of this design. To Yolngu, the composition poses a number of questions. Can non-Aboriginal Australians fulfill a role similar to that played by the whale hunter? Can there be equality before the law?

It was the historical relationship between Yolngu and Sama-Bajau that inspired Burrumarra to think in terms of joint management for the Arafura Sea, with each party contributing special skills, interests, and histories. He described the relationship in this way: "What the whale hunter does with his spear, we do with *yidaki, bilma,* and *mani-kay.*"[27] In other words, they both followed the one law, the law of the sea, but from "different sides." Burrumarra's feelings were also summed up in his memorable statement that "What gold is to the land, the whale is to the sea." With these words, he was asserting the view that the material and social benefits that non-Aborigines enjoy as a result of the exploitation of Aboriginal land in the form of mining have their equivalent in ritual practice associated with belief in the whale. The Yolngu and whale-hunter approach to the sea was spiritually based, whereas non-Aboriginal interests were primarily economic. Belief in the whale, the highest of sea totems and most redolent with meaning, was the foundation of the wealth of sea people, Burrumarra asserted.

A PROPOSAL FOR YOLNGU MANAGEMENT OF THE SEA

Under provisions of the Fisheries Act (NT) Aboriginal people may utilize the seas for sustenance purposes only. Species that are important in a religious and economic sense, such as the barramundi or mackerel, cannot be caught for profit, whereas nonpreservable fish, like the mullet or catfish, legally may be gathered and resold within the community. Even then, however, the Yolngu must hold a government-issued license. Burrumarra believed that these restrictions should not apply, and that coastal Aboriginal communities should be involved in the fishing industry. Further, all matters to do with the sea should be the subject of consultations, with the Yolngu playing an active role in the management of resources.

It was in recognition of Burrumarra's work in the fight for Aboriginal sea rights that a new generation of Aborigines at Elcho Is-

---

27. Didjeridu, clapsticks and song

land launched an indigenous marine protection strategy for the Arafura Sea, called *Manbuynga ga Rulyapa* in the Yolngu languages. According to Burrumarra's son, Terry Yumbulul, it was the Warramiri leader's wish that such rights be acknowledged by government. A participant in negotiations leading to the proclamation of the Aboriginal Land Rights Act (NT), Burrumarra was disappointed that Yolngu ownership under this legislation was to extend only as far as the shoreline. This meant that Aborigines would have no way of enforcing their time-honored practices, as they are now able to do on land. They have to stand by and watch as the by-catch from prawn trawlers and tuna boats washes in on the tide, and stocks of totemically significant sea life are increasingly depleted.

A draft proposal for the management of *Manbuynga ga Rulyapa* was released by the Ginytjirrang Mala (steering committee) at a press conference held during Burrumarra's funeral. The following recommendations were laid out:

• Australian maps should refer to the area in question as Manbuynga ga Rulyapa.

• Australian governments should consult with Yolngu about Aboriginal interests in the sea.

• A bilateral comanagement arrangement with Indonesia should be pursued by the Australian government and Yolngu.

• The marine strategy should be based on Yolngu management principles.

• There should be government recognition of Yolngu sea laws.

• The Yolngu should set minimum safety standards for ships traversing *Manbuynga ga Rulyapa.*

• Yolngu should own and operate their own fishing enterprises.

• Mining proposals for the sea should proceed according to Yolngu law.

The Ginydjirrang Mala is a self-appointed group representing all Yolngu interests, and is heavily weighted with Warramiri clan members and representatives from the Dhuwa moiety Djambarrpuyngu (Wutjara) clan. Led by Burrumarra's son Terry Yumbulul and Dhuwa leader Keith Djiniyini, it also includes members of the Ritharrngu, Wangurri, Galpu, Gumatj, and Gupapuyngu clans. Initial funding was received from the Ocean Rescue 2000 program for the Ginydjirrang Mala to design and promote a management plan for the Arafura Sea that would utilize both local Aboriginal and non-Aboriginal expertise. The agenda was the education of the Australian public with regard to Yolngu interests in Manbuynga ga Rulyapa and to encourage Arnhem Land community members to progressively reassume responsibility for various levels of sea management, based on customary law.

Clans living along the coastal fringes, groups such as the Wangurri and Datiwuy, possess expertise in mangrove habitats and their maintenance, whereas coral reef and open-sea protection is a task the Warramiri set for themselves, with assistance from the Gumatj. Inland groups such as the Ritharrngu also have much to offer on the subject of freshwater availability and the effects of erosion or fertilizer runoff. This vast store of Yolngu knowledge is yet to be tapped. Only in the past five years, for instance, have chemical companies begun to negotiate deals with Aboriginal groups about their use of traditional medicines. Commonly found plant foods such as the bush grape, *Mundjutj*, has a very concentrated supply of Vitamin C, and Yolngu have long recognized and utilized its potential for dealing with various symptoms. Other traditional remedies are being investigated. For instance, Yolngu freely acknowledge that they have only part of the answer regarding the active ingredient formed by crushing and swallowing green ants as a means of fighting head colds.

THE NEED FOR A STRATEGY

The United Nations Food and Agriculture Organization in 1994 declared that all the world's fish stocks were in serious decline and most of the larger marine ecosystems such as Australia's Great Barrier Reef were showing signs of pollution-related stress (Ginydjirrang Mala 1994). Australia's northern neighbor, Indonesia, has a transmigration policy and as many as 150,000 people per year are being relocated in the less populated regions of Maluku and Irian, which border the Arafura Sea. These are but two of a number of compelling reasons for the need for a comprehensive marine protection strategy for the Arafura Sea. As the report of the Ginydjirrang Mala declares:

> [In 1996 *Yolngu*] witnessed...hundreds of dead beached whales;...endangered species of turtles, dugong and crocodiles trapped in nets; marine pollution; and illegal fishing by foreign boats.[28] We do not want to see our food supply disappear, our beaches polluted or our sacred sites desecrated. The fish we are catching now, even with modern boats and tackle, are getting smaller. Oysters near Gove are already showing the effects of poisoning from anti-fouling on yachts moored there and are unfit for human consumption. We

---

28. Ninety-eight Indonesian and two Taiwanese boats were apprehended in Australian waters in 1996.

want to be able to continue to pass on our culture, knowledge and traditions and our marine resources to our children, but...outside pressures threaten this.

Another reason for a strategy is the amount of money currently being spent in detecting, detaining, or otherwise dealing with the increasing number of illegal fishermen operating in north Australia. Ginydjirrang Mala spokespersons Yumbulul and Djiniyini (1996:108–109) have this solution:

> The...coast of Arnhem Land faces the most heavily populated group of islands in the world.... The amount of rubbish that drifts down onto our shores with the north-westerly monsoons is enormous. Overfishing is occurring from both the Australian fishery and as a result of foreign boats operating illegally in our waters.... [W]hat needs to be set up is a bi-lateral co-management arrangement between the Australian Government and the Federal Republic of Indonesia for the whole of Manbuynga ga Rulyapa. Yolngu want to be a part of that agreement and have a strong say in how it is set up and managed. We are willing to travel to Indonesia and talk with fishing folk there to tell them our concerns and to listen to theirs.

Management of the Arafura Sea is currently based on Australian intergovernmental arrangements through the Offshore Constitutional Settlement Act 1978. This operates within an international framework of treaties associated with the law of the sea (Ginydjirrang Mala 1994). The writers of the Indigenous Marine Protection Strategy are critical of this management regime, saying,

> Since Federation...marine resources management practices have been characterized by meager funding and poor science. Government and industry co-management have failed to prevent over-fishing and the virtual extermination in some places of native fish stocks like abalone, tuna and shark. This history...means that Australian communities must now either actively participate in the protection of their own vulnerable local marine resources or watch them disappear.

Yumbulul says that Yolngu are no longer content to sit by and watch this happen. Indigenous management practices are ceremonially based and enforced by a strict local permit and zoning system. Non-Aboriginal Australians need to understand and follow this system, Yumbulul argues. Yolngu desire to have all fishing activity in Manbuynga ga Rulyapa put under their control and want to participate in the overhauling of fisheries legislation. The aim is to achieve the implementation of a regionalization policy in fisheries management which could become a model for marine resource management in other areas of Australia.

Progress to Date

The Northern Land Council (NLC) is a body established under the auspices of the Land Rights Act to ascertain and express the wishes of Aboriginal landowners; protect sacred sites; negotiate with bodies desiring to establish enterprises on Aboriginal land; and assist Aborigines in claiming land and sea rights. The NLC's response to the launch of the marine strategy has been threefold: (1) Anthropologists have been engaged to investigate Aboriginal beliefs concerning sea rights along the Northern Territory coast; (2) in 1995 a conference was organized to facilitate discussion between Government Fisheries representatives, the Commercial Fishing Association, and Aboriginal leaders from across the north coast; and (3) in 1998 the NLC sued the Northern Territory director of fisheries seeking to make travel through the inter-tidal zone adjacent to Aboriginal-owned land an act of trepass. Still under deliberation, the success of this court case would mean that fishermen will be required to seek the permission of Aboriginal landowners for access to Aboriginal-controlled waters up to the low watermark.

The federal government has responded to some of the issues raised by the steering committee in that there are now two Commonwealth Inter-Departmental Committees (IDCs) working toward developing marine-related policies. One is concerned with illegal Indonesian fishing and the other ocean policy development.

Progress towards the implementation of an indigenous marine strategy however has been slow. The only tangible evidence of change in the past two years has been that Aboriginal people are now represented on several regional Northern Territory fishing committees. As Yumbulul and Djiniyini (1996:109) complain:

> The Northern Territory Fisheries Council...always responds to our calls for joint management by saying "hey, we are more than willing to consult with you in formulating our policies. What more do you want? But they fail to grasp the big picture.... The whole north coast is being fished out and polluted at an alarming rate and we as a community must act now.

Despite a cautious and limited response by government, the Ginydjirrang Mala has continued to lobby for the recognition of their rights and has traveled widely in Australia to places such as the Torres Strait, Townsville, and Canberra to speak about shared responsibilities and concerns. Within Yolngu communities, they have been involved in a public education campaign to teach Yolngu about the need to protect and properly manage the sea. Committee members have also embarked upon both air and sea excursions to record sacred sites in the waters far north of Arnhem Land with the intention of having these protected under Australian Heritage legislation as sites of national significance.

Native Title and Sea Rights

Up until 1998, the Native Title Act had the potential to extend the recognition of Aboriginal sea interests to a form of ownership. However, the federal government's 1998 amendments disallow all such claims. Yolngu leader and Chairman of the Northern Land Council Galarrwuy Yunupingu, a strong supporter of the Manbuynga ga Rulyapa proposal, has said he would veto any talks with government officials on native title or reconciliation until such time as they demonstrated a willingness to comprehend what native title means to Yolngu. Mr Yunupingu suggested that politicians need to see a Yolngu ceremony in "full swing" and added that native title was not about "whitefella paper." "It is the customary law and customary system which still governs us and gives us the rights to survive and live." These rights, he said, could not be legislated away by anyone.

Yumbulul and Djiniyini see Yolngu custodianship of the sea as being a basic human right, as identified in the various United Nations proclamations on cultural survival to which Australia is a signatory. Their hope is that in the longer term, the recognition of native title by non-Aboriginal Australians will enable Yolngu people to negotiate joint management and commercial arrangements regarding the use of their seas.

There are compelling reasons warranting a comprehensive marine protection strategy for the Arafura Sea. Environmental survival is one. Cultural survival is another. What the Yolngu propose is the utilization of both Aboriginal and non-Aboriginal expertise in meeting the challenge. In fact it is a precondition for reconciliation that Yolngu progressively reassume responsibility for various levels of sea management.

10

Mining, Marginalization, and the Power of Veto

Virtually the only time when non-Aboriginal Australians come face to face with Aborigines is when development companies and, by proxy, thousands of their shareholders lobby for access to Aboriginal land. Mining is the foundation for Australia's claim to developed nation status, and the commonest forum having a bearing on the reconciliation debate is the Northern Territory mining meeting. Powerful arguments for reconciliation, such as pay-your-own-way and equality-before-the-law, come into play both inside and outside these sessions, and these claims vie with those by Aborigines and their supporters for justice-before-reconciliation. Both sides stress the need to build a future together as a single nation.

Aboriginal freehold title in the Northern Territory is the strongest form of land tenure that Australia's indigenous people enjoy. While the Land Rights Act enjoins Aborigines to meet regularly with developers, the landowners have the power of veto over development. Control of Aboriginal land by Aborigines appears to provide an opportunity for economic development to proceed at a pace acceptable to Aborigines. But the current methodology utilized in pursuing a decision favors the would-be miners, and although Aboriginal land councils such as the NLC attempt to ensure that Aborigines are in control, such is not always the case.

The past five years has witnessed the development of a trend in Aborigines saying yes to mining exploration on their country. In this chapter, I speculate upon the reasons for this trend and examine the logistical and political circumstances under which Aborigines make these decisions. I detail a range of case studies from Arnhem Land, including an example from Galiwin'ku that involves the Warramiri and draws on the Birrinydji legacy. I conclude that securing a "yes" decision from Aboriginal landowners (traditional owners or T.O.'s in the terminology of the Land Rights Act) is tantamount to a card game in which the odds are stacked in favor of developers. Aborigines respond to the playing conditions in ways which sometimes result in a stalemate, but there is little prospect of initiating development on their own terms.

THE DILEMMA OF MINING

The Aboriginal Land Rights Act offers traditional owners no choice with regard to whether or not they will consider mining on their country. According to the terms of the Act, they must respond to requests for meetings with company representatives at least every five years. If the landowners exercise their powers of veto, then a company has the right to come back and ask again, which many traditional owners find exasperating. This "humbug" causes considerable community friction, for at each meeting, some individuals will always be in favor, others will strongly oppose it, while the majority will not be sure. By far the most common reason given by Aborigines for saying yes to a development proposal is "to get miners off their backs."

In an ideal world, support for development proposals on Aboriginal land would come from Aborigines themselves. *They* would be the ones to initiate discussions with developers or embark on projects of their own choosing in their own time, whether it be mining, tourism, fishing, pastoral activities, and so on. They would not only have access to, but a comprehensive understanding of, information relating to the potential impacts of the development. As a group they would delineate areas of land suitable for an agreed project from within their clan territories and, with the support of other potentially affected Aboriginal peoples and legal or anthropological support from bodies such as land councils, negotiate directly with the companies of their choice. They would enter into contracts with developers as equal partners, be employed in the ventures, and monitor the progress of the projects through to their completion.

This was Burrumarra's vision in the 1950s, when the Warramiri first came into contact with developers. Isolated areas on the Wessel Islands were to be opened for bauxite mining, and Galiwin'ku Yolngu negotiated a 25 percent share of all profits. The deal fell through, however, because of a lack of suitable port facilities and the discovery of even richer mineral deposits in the vicinity of the Yirrkala mission that became the site of the Nabalco alumina refinery and the township of Gove.

The destruction of Aboriginal sacred sites at Gove and the indifference the miners demonstrated toward the Aborigine's fate has soured ambitions concerning mining. Yolngu know of huge deposits of minerals on their land but have been quite content to let them sit. From 1976 to 1985, when Aborigines in the Northern Territory first gained the power to give or withhold consent over development projects, they blocked virtually all mining exploration projects submitted to them. The reason for the denials is a much debated topic, but it is obviously linked to years and years of no consultations and the initiation of projects against Aboriginal wishes. Added to this was concern about deleterious effects to the environment, the social impact of royalty distributions, and devious tactics by miners.

There is no doubt that more and more Aborigines wish to obtain access to the economic benefits of mining. They wish to be freed from over-dependency on welfare and government handouts. Over the past ten years there has also been a discernable improvement in the attitude of mining companies toward the Aboriginal Land Rights Act and toward negotiating with Aborigines. Rather than fighting for changes to the legislation, companies now work with Aborigines in order to broker a deal. Despite this, Northern Territory government continues to apply pressure on the federal government to legislatively remove the powers of consent that Northern Territory Aborigines presently enjoy. The three large mines now operating in the "Top End" of the Northern Territory, (the Ranger uranium mine in west Arnhem Land, the Nabalco bauxite mine at Gove, and the Gemco manganese mine on Groote Eylandt), were all established against the wishes of Aborigines in the days prior to the enactment of land rights legislation. The Northern Territory government wishes for a return to the days when they could "steamroller" developments they believed to be in the national interest. The desire is to see either the dilution of the powers that Aborigines enjoy as property owners under the Land Rights Act, or the replacement of this legislation by the Native Title Act.

THE PLAYING FIELD

One of the few forums where Aborigines speak from a position of power, namely the present-day mining meeting, is a post-1976 phenomenon. The Aboriginal Land Rights (NT) Act section 48AA(4)a, establishes that:

> A Land Council shall not enter into an agreement [with a mining company]...in respect of an area of land unless it is satisfied that: the traditional Aboriginal owners of the land understand the nature and purpose of the agreement and, as a group, consent to it.

Mining companies wanting access to Aboriginal land in the Northern Territory must first apply for an exploration license (ELA) from the Northern Territory Mines Department. After being offered particular blocks of land, the Aboriginal Land Rights Act then requires the company to submit a proposal to the land council, who notifies the traditional Aboriginal landowners and other interested Aboriginal parties. Until 1987, Aborigines could say yes to exploration but subsequently no to mining if minerals were found, but, following significant pressure by mining companies seeking security of tenure, the Aboriginal Land Rights Act was amended. If Aborigines now say yes to exploration, they cannot at a later point say no to mining. Despite this, since 1991 there has been a considerable number of mining agreements entered into between Aborigines and mining companies in Arnhem Land, and Aborigines have been able to demand and obtain:

> …both substantial royalty payments and direct involvement in economic activities associated with mining such as employment and training on site, provision of goods and services, taking of equity in mining and related projects, (O'Faircheallaigh 1995:3)

The NLC's approach in negotiating agreements on behalf of the traditional Aboriginal landowners ensures that Aborigines receive maximum benefits from mining activity while minimizing negative impacts. In most cases the NLC negotiates a package that delivers benefits at both the exploration and mining stage. During exploration, a small sum is paid to the traditional Aboriginal owners for compensation for damage and disturbance to the land. At the mining stage, the financial package may take a variety of forms, including royalty payments, rentals, net profit interest, and so on. Should the mining company invite the traditional owners to acquire equity in the project, Aborigines form their own corporation and sign a joint venture contract with the miners. The agreement usually contains specific provisions relating to employment opportunities, training programs, local community infrastructure and, the protection of significant or sacred sites.

Decision-Making Circumstances

Prior to a mining meeting, anthropological research is conducted in order to try to determine who has interests in the land in question. A major problem is that ELA mining tenements rarely, if ever, involve a single clan group. In most cases the boundaries, as conceived by officers of the Northern Territory Mines Department, cut through the territories of a considerable number of sometimes unrelated clans. Members of these clans will have ceremonial, family, or other relations with clans outside the mining tenement area leading to a situation in which it is sometimes very unclear how widely consultations should be conducted. At the same time, the success of a meeting depends on there being full representation.

In many Aboriginal communities, meetings are becoming a daily occurrence, so few people bother to show up despite the letters, public broadcasts on local radio and television stations, and personal approaches by land council and liaison staff. The creation of ELA tenements that divide a clan's territory into several parts for which different mining companies have an interest makes the situation unnecessarily complex. The end result is that the same people must attend a seemingly endless series of meetings. If Aborigines refuse to give consent to a project or even to negotiate, the ELA is held in abeyance for five years. The mining company does not lose the right to negotiate in the future, however, and can come back indefinitely at each five year interval.

Aboriginal groups know that some companies have poor records in both environmental management and in their dealings with indigenous people. The only weapon they possess if such a company approaches them is to refuse consent to negotiate. They cannot approach a more suitable corporation if they are seeking development. Some companies may offer traditional owners an unreasonable deal and be sure of a refusal. They thus keep their ELA for another five years recurring. This suits a company if the market is low and they are spending their exploration budget elsewhere, or if they have other priorities. This is called "warehousing" and is illegal as it effectively excludes any competition from Aboriginal land. There is no mechanism by which Aboriginal people can rid themselves of such a company. Aboriginal groups wanting to initiate exploration on their land are therefore powerless. The public perception, however, is that Aborigines are preventing or delaying development.

ABORIGINAL RESPONSES

Many Arnhemlanders believe that saying yes to mining companies means another white town, loss of control over land, and the poisoning of rivers and estuaries. Yet it is often said by Aborigines that if the mining company demonstrates a sensitivity to Aboriginal aspirations, and a willingness to understand the struggles in which they are engaged, and share equally in the wealth generated from mining on Aboriginal land, then an affirmative answer to their request would not be uncommon.

From an Aboriginal viewpoint, mining companies have vast amounts of money, and they want to generate more from Aboriginal land. Some Aborigines associate mining with complete and utter degradation of land and self. Yet at mining meetings there is almost always the universal cry by the elders for unity between peoples and an end to the divisions that keep one group locked into poverty on the margins of white society. On this basis, some Aborigines appear willing to enter into partnerships with the mining companies, but only if the protection of sacred sites is guaranteed and Aboriginal rights respected. Such partnerships are seen as being based on sharing equally in the profits of a venture, but to date negotiated mining agreements rarely result in anything more than a 2 percent share for Aborigines. The following case studies represent a range of outcomes at mining meetings attended by the author between 1995 and 1997.

Case Studies

Aborigines often give a decision very quickly, for they have already made up their minds about a project. In one case study from northwest Arnhem Land, a spokesperson for the ten assembled clans vetoed the proposal, saying, "They are playing games. They don't give a [damn] about us. How can we do anything for them?" The T.O.'s had no hesitation in foregoing potential royalties as a way of asserting their own dignity as a people. They would keep the land untouched by miners, even if it meant they would continue to be poor.

A commonly expressed view at a "yes" meeting, however, is that people are impatient for development and they expect to become rich overnight. There is sometimes a feeling of euphoria when the old men give their consent to a project, though there is a less than 1 percent chance of a company finding a mineable quantity of ore. All that the traditional owners will receive, in all probability, is an annual compensation distribution for the period of exploration. When divided between members of an average-sized clan (say 50 people), this may be as little as $200 per person per annum.

Clan members often feel pressured into saying yes. At one meeting in west Arnhem Land, the clan spokesperson said that she was sick and tired of miners coming back every five years "humbugging" her. It made her feel sorry to think of the loss incurred in the transition from bush life to community living. But she added that her old father had said yes to mining exploration and she had to follow his wishes. By saying yes the humbug would stop.

Sometimes the power of veto is taken from the hands of landowners. In a case study from Galiwin'ku, all the Yolngu had agreed to mineral exploration but had held off giving a final decision until they had slept on it. That night, the senior Aborigine from Howard Island had a dream in which a sacred object hidden in the bush, representing the spirit of the place to be affected by the development, "stood up" and made its presence felt. The dreamer interpreted this as opposition to mining. At the meeting the following morning the spokesperson said, "We all agree to mining, but the country says no."

In west Arnhem Land there were a number of situations where the last surviving members of Aboriginal populations made statements about what they wanted for the future. For instance the last member of a particular clan stated, "While I'm alive, there'll be no mining. When I'm dead you can mine." At another meeting, a substantial cash offer was made to one of the last members of another clan group to agree to mining on his estate. While understandably lured by this, he wanted his land to be made into a national park so that it would never be mined.

In a further case study, the clan spokesperson admitted to having no detailed knowledge of the countryside or its sacred sites. He said that the old people had all died and the current generation was uncomfortable with the pressure being applied for them to say yes or no. His decision to say no was part of a broader plan to learn about the country and to consolidate his clan's relationship with it. In a separate meeting over this same tenement, the spokesperson said "We are holding the land through non-Aboriginal law and not Aboriginal law. But still we are trying to maintain Aboriginal law. We don't want mining."

BURRUMARRA, MACASSANS, AND MINING IN NORTHEAST ARNHEM LAND

The Warramiri clan as a whole has been steadfast in its opposition to mining since 1976. While Burrumarra always agreed in principle, he bowed to the pressure of numbers. The destruction of sacred sites in Gove, even 20 years previously, was reason enough. But in 1988, eighty years after the end of the Macassan era, Burrumarra promoted the view amongst those who would listen that mining on his land at Dholtji would help restore wealth and status to Aboriginal people—a wealth and status that had been usurped first by itinerant voyagers from Sulawesi and then by European colonists. For the aging Aboriginal leader there were no doubts. Mining was a part of Aboriginal history and it was an avenue to the good life. Since time immemorial, coastal hematite outcrops had been transformed into iron-bladed tools by Yolngu working under the guidance of Birrinydji. Following first contact, Yolngu "lost" the skills and technologies of the modern world. Burrumarra sought a return to this precontact golden era.

Although close family did not question his authority as the spokesperson for the clan or Birrinydji, some Yolngu believed he was attempting to sell off the country to Balanda for his own personal gain. Others saw his views on the past as anachronistic and they objected to mining exploration, even though the land in question was sacred to the memory of a "timeless" partnership that was once thought to have existed between Aborigines and non-Aborigines through Birrinydji and Walitha'walitha.

Burrumarra's Dream

In the weeks following consent to exploration in the vicinity of the Dholtji outstation, Burrumarra had a dream which sparked considerable local discussion. In the dream Burrumarra's younger brothers Liwukang and Wulanybuma were clearing land for an airstrip at this ceremonial center for Birrinydji. In complying with Burrumarra's wish, the brothers were planning to make Dholtji the large settlement that it had been in the days of the Macassans. It was here that British explorer Matthew Flinders encountered the Macassan fleet in 1803 (Flinders 1814) and here also that anthropologists Berndt and Berndt (1954) describe great festivities taking place on shore as up to sixty praus and a thousand men reconnoitered prior to their return to Sulawesi. The brothers had nearly finished the airstrip when their bulldozer was halted by an obstacle. It was a huge gold nugget. "This must belong to Birrinydji," they thought and went off to get their older brother. The Warramiri leader stared at the find and understood that the wealth of whites could be theirs once again, and he reflected on the past. Birrinydji was the rich minerals of the earth, the transformed hematite, the source of the technology that made foreigners wealthy, allowing them to dominate Aborigines. And he bent down to pick up the prize, and as he lifted it and held it in his arms, Birrinydji, Burrumarra's Aboriginality and his Dreaming went into the ground and out of his life. He had the wealth of the Balanda and that was all that he had. The Yolngu interpreted his dream to mean that to savage the earth for its "spirit," as in mining, was to lose one's identity and become like the Balanda. By resisting the temptation one would maintain one's Aboriginality but also one's poverty.

The Evidence for Iron-Making

The tales of Birrinydji demonstrate a history of mining among the Warramiri. Nevertheless, despite Yolngu legends, there is no hard evidence of Aboriginal iron-making in precolonial Australia. The literature suggests only that a major outcome of the Macassan period was an appreciation of iron's unique qualities and it became a highly prized item of trade (Warner 1969:450; Macknight 1972:305). The tomahawk and knife, the detachable harpoon head, shovel-nose metal spear, and the small metal bowl used in long wooden smoking pipes were particularly valued items.

But it is possible that Arnhem Land was a source of raw material for local and overseas iron production? The process of iron manufacture does not require elaborate machinery. Any place where raw materials are available will suffice. In fact, techniques which might have been practiced in Arnhem Land in the past are still carried on throughout eastern Indonesia today. While Macknight's (1976) detailed study of the Macassan trepang industry casts doubt on such speculation, one could certainly imagine situations where it might have become a necessity: For example, if an anchor was lost at sea or if nails were required to repair the praus and there were no other craft in the vicinity to lend assistance or finished materials. How else can one explain the Warramiri leader's detailed knowledge of the iron-making process? For instance Burrumarra claims that:

> Birrinydji used the "red rock" from the beach...Rratjpa is intelligence for all mankind, the source of wealth and power of Balanda and Yolngu—from it comes all the technology—axes, knives and hammers.

Mining on Aboriginal Land

Despite the legacy of Birrinydji, mining is not an option for a majority of Yolngu and, especially in the Gove/Yirrkala area, the very idea of non-Aboriginal companies drilling on Yolngu land evokes a deep bitterness. Some see Birrinydji, and consequently their Aboriginality, as being vulnerable to such desecration. This fear of mining by Yolngu is well documented. In relation to a traditional bark painting by Burrumarra's brother Liwukang depicting Birrinydji with the metal tools of his trade, Cawte (1993:68) asks:

> Warramiri contemplating Birrinydji are supposed to ponder why their "iron age" was lost.... Does an iron age destroy itself because mining violates the earth?

While Burrumarra linked the extraction of bauxite and the production of alumina at the Nabalco plant at Gove with Birrinydji's iron-making, he opposed this mine from the outset because of the developer's failure to consult with Yolngu (see McIntosh 1994:23). Yet as far back as the 1940s, Burrumarra and the Wangurri leader Badangga were prospecting for diamonds on their land. In the case of proposed mineral exploration at Dholtji in 1988, while Burrumarra's dream did not change his feelings on pushing ahead with the project, his family, in consultation with anthropologists, marked off so much of the exploration zone as sacred and "no-go" areas that it was no longer feasible for the company to proceed. The new generation did not contest the Warramiri leader's wishes. They had merely ensured the integrity of their sacred areas.

For a range of reasons, many of which are connected to the Dreaming, Burrumarra's answer to developers requesting access to his country was usually yes, even though the history of race relations in northeast Arnhem Land worked against his wish. The people, as a whole, would say no to him. But the "fact" of iron-making on remote Arnhem Land beaches provided an alternative to the sharply contrasting views on mining, namely that saying yes means selling out one's inheritance (as when Birrinydji went into the ground in Burrumarra's dream), while saying no results in the maintenance of cultural difference and poverty. For Burrumarra, mining on Aboriginal terms would mean one could be wealthy and simultaneously maintain one's sense of identity and power. To him, this was a legacy of Birrinydji.

WHOSE INTERESTS ARE BEING SERVED?

Despite twenty years of land rights in the Northern Territory and powers under the Act that no other Aboriginal groups in Australia enjoy, traditional owners are not in a position to initiate mining on their land. Their powers are negative only: They can say no and block proposals. In case studies detailed in this chapter, we see the full gamut of reactions to the rules of the game as played in the Northern Territory. We have responses emphasizing the need to protect country from outside intrusion, to more fatalistic responses, to the desire to profit from one's land, but only if the financial return is immediate and substantial. Aborigines are willing to enter into negotiations with miners, but the pain of dispossession and the continuing indifference of whites, who grow wealthy at Aboriginal expense, manifests itself in the decision-making process. Clan groups continue to die out evoking a deep sense of resentment towards intruders. In 1989, the last member of the Djambarrpuyngu-Djadaya clan of Elcho Island died. In 1993 the Lamamirri clan, a Birrinydji group, became extinct. Burrumarra's mother was the last surviving member of the Brarrngu clan of Rarragala Island, and she died in the 1950s. All of these territories are "no-go" areas in terms of development, out of respect for the dead, but this doesn't stop developers from asking.

In making a decision about mining, traditional owners must think about, and make statements on, the contemporary nature of their own identity as Aborigines and their marginalization as a community in relation to non-Aborigines. The trend in saying yes is in part a reflection of the confidence that people feel about the act. Aborigines accept or reject a deal on its merits, as is their right. They have no hesitation in negotiating a deal with miners so long as it is a fair one. But the trend is also a response to the fact that Aborigines are becoming more and more reliant on the monetary economy and they are saying yes to mining because of their growing need for cash. The act allows companies to keep coming back every five years and Aborigines know that their lives are changing and that sooner or later they will give in to the repeated requests, if only as a means of getting by. Mining is an ever-present option, and while it is the way of the Warramiri ancestors, it cannot be condoned if it leads to the desecration of sacred Dreaming sites.

A common response is for people to say yes to mining, but only if it is right now. The old people living in tin shacks, who are rained on each wet season, the ones who really know about the country—they must benefit. This is how many of the younger generation justify their decision to consent to exploration and mining. Alternatively, some members of the older generation do not trust today's youth, believing they will "sell off the country" given the chance, and they want to be in a position to control proceedings. The change since the early 1990s is a reflection of a fatalistic attitude to life evident in communities like Galiwin'ku. There is no tomorrow. Non-Aborigines will have their way and Aborigines want what is theirs, now. This is the social impact of the act in its current form, and the principal cause of the trend towards "yes" decisions.

However, the increasing number of development approvals is also evidence of a trend toward reconciliation. Aborigines are prepared to pay their own way and desire economic self-sufficiency. But there is one condition. Birrinydji provides the Warramiri with an attitude shared by almost all clans in Arnhem Land: non-Aborigines must understand that their continued well-being depends on the exploitation of Aboriginal land. There is no possible justification for removing the powers of veto that Aborigines currently enjoy, unless of course the Northern Territory government openly admits that it represents the interests of mining companies and is willing to disregard the well-being of the 25 percent of its population who are of Aboriginal descent. Only by acknowledging the rightful status of Aborigines as landowners and working together with a view to building partnerships will reconciliation be an achievable goal.

Reconciliation on the World Stage

When Aborigines travel overseas they are often greeted as visiting dignitaries, as members of their own sovereign nations, particularly by other Fourth World peoples. But they return home to uncertain futures and low status. Tasmanian Aboriginal activist Michael Mansell ventured abroad in the 1980s, on a homemade Aboriginal passport which was only reluctantly recognized by Australian immigration agents. Star Aboriginal athlete Cathy Freeman completed a victory lap adorned with both the Australian and the Aboriginal flag when she won the gold medal in the women's 400-meter at the Commonwealth Games in 1994 and was threatened with dismissal from the team. Noel Fatnowna, a spokesperson for Queensland's Kanak population, was treated as a Pacific Islander diplomat on arrival at a chic hotel in Townsville until he was asked which group of islands he represented and replied that he had been born and still lived in the shanty town on the banks of the local river.

The international arena has become an avenue for the pursuit of Aboriginal reconciliation. Australia is a signatory to a number of international covenants involving indigenous rights, and Aborigines are asserting their claim for rights before United Nations forums in New York and Geneva. At the 1997 Australian Reconciliation Convention, Professor James Anaya reported on the leadership role of Aborigines in the pursuit for widespread recognition of indigenous languages, cultures, and traditions, and for the achievement of autonomy and self-management, free from undue interference from central governments.

Attempts by Aborigines to assert themselves as a sovereign people on the domestic front are, however, thwarted by both the legacy of *terra nullius* and the vagaries of domestic politics. The Gove bauxite mine, for instance, was established without concern for the wishes of Yolngu and northeast Arnhem Land Aborigines are now pursuing compensation from the responsible multinational corporation. In 1996, Australia tried to enter the European Union and Yolngu were at the forefront of attempts to dissuade the Europeans from permitting admission. Part of a strategy to have the government rethink its native title amendments, it was also an attempt to alert Europeans to the treatment of Yolngu by the Swiss mining company that operates Nabalco.

In this chapter I provide examples of Yolngu involvement on the world stage, and, for such small communities, these examples can only be described as remarkable. One is the international delegations lobbying for the recognition of the human rights of indigenous people, and the performance to worldwide audiences of protest songs like "Treaty" by acclaimed musicians, *Yothu Yindi*. The other involves religious and ceremonial expeditions, such as the noteworthy travels of the Galiwin'ku Black Crusade to Germany, Israel, Indonesia, and New Zealand, and the organization by the Warramiri and Gumatj of an innovative ceremonial dance exchange commemorating a shared past with Macassans.

INTERNATIONAL COVENANTS

In ratifying international conventions, such as the International Covenant on Economic, Social and Cultural Rights (ICESCR), Australia has agreed to ensure compliance, and has assured the international community that the principles of these provisions will be reflected in the lives of all citizens. It has also agreed to report regularly to the committees on the degree of compliance. But, to date, Gumatj Yolngu leader and Northern Land Council Chairperson Galarrwuy Yunupingu asserts that these covenants have meant little to Australia's indigenous people, and the Australian government has ignored its obligations.

In 1995, Australia proposed the development of a framework for bilateral trade and economic cooperation with the European Union. In January 1997, talks stalled when Australia refused to sign the proposed trade agreement because it contained human rights provisions. Article 1, for instance, declares that respect for democratic principles and basic human rights, as proclaimed in the Universal Declaration of Human Rights, underpins the internal and international policies of the union and of Australia and constitutes an essential element of this agreement.

Yunupingu urged the federal government to reconsider its decision, both for the sake of Australia's international reputation and in order to reassure indigenous people that their human rights were safeguarded. He was deeply concerned about this refusal, as it signaled a movement away from international and domestic human rights standards. In a Northern Land Council media release dated January 31, 1997, Mr. Yunupingu declared:

The European Parliament should know that the Australian Government is demonstrating scant regard for the human rights of Indigenous Australians. The Australian Government will happily trample over Indigenous rights to enable the Australian rural and pastoral and resource extraction industries to get on with business at our expense.

According to the Yolngu leader, Australia is in breach of international obligations with respect to citizenship rights. Amendments to the Native Title Act have violated Aboriginal property rights under the Universal Declaration on Human Rights. They also contravene Australia's own Racial Discrimination Act, enacted to comply with this covenant.

The International Bill of Rights is composed of the Universal Declaration on Human Rights, the International Covenant on Economic, Social and Cultural Rights (ICESCR) and the International Covenant on Civil and Political Rights (ICCPR). The ICESCR came into force in Australia in 1976 and the ICCPR in 1981. Under the terms of these covenants, Australia is obliged to report regularly to the respective U.N. committees, but both periodic reports are well overdue. Both covenants guarantee equal rights and adequate protection against discrimination, but Yunupingu says that there has been a failure to overcome structural discrimination and the barriers to gaining full access to and equity in the range of available government services such as provision of education and health services, water, and electricity to many indigenous communities. The treatment of Aborigines by the justice system is in breach of the ICCPR, and the U.S. State Department was critical of Australia's response to Aboriginal deaths in custody in its 1996 human rights report. In addition, Article 27 states that minorities shall not be denied the right to enjoy their own culture, to profess and practice their own religion, or to use their own language, yet, said Yunupingu, the continued desecration of sacred sites by developers is often based on the refusal of courts to acknowledge Aboriginal land- and sea-based spiritual beliefs.

Australia has recently recognized the authority of the United Nations committees to receive communications from individual Australians claiming their rights under ICCPR, as well as under the Convention on the Elimination of All Forms of Racial Discrimination (CERD) and the Convention Against Torture and Other Cruel, Inhuman and Degrading Treatment and Punishment (CAT). Indigenous Australians are only just beginning to make effective use of these procedures.

THE YOLNGU DELEGATION TO SWITZERLAND

Galarrwuy Yunupingu had an additional incentive for trying to ensure Australia's compliance with human rights provisions in the European Union trade agreement. It was the European multinational corporation, Alusuisse-Lonza, operating under the name of Nabalco in Australia, that devastated his homeland in the 1960s and continues to ignore Yolngu demands for reasonable compensation. Yolngu never gave permission for bauxite to be mined in northeast Arnhem Land. As Yunupingu cried:

> I saw the bulldozers rip through our Gumatj country. I watched my father stand in front of the bulldozers to stop them clearing sacred trees and chase away the drivers with an ax. I watched him crying when our sacred waterhole was bulldozed. It was one of our Dreamings and a source of our water. I saw a township wreck our beautiful homeland forever. I saw my father suffering physically when this was happening and he never forgave Alusuisse-Lonza for what they did.

In 1963 the Australian government made a unilateral decision to excise land from the Arnhem Land Aboriginal Reserve for mining enterprises and, in 1969, Alusuisse-Lonza entered into an agreement with the government in which they were given unlimited access to the bauxite reserves on that land. The Aboriginal protest and court case has been described in previous chapters, but although it led to the proclamation of the Land Rights Act, it has not ensured a fair deal for Yolngu.

The Nabalco mine earns the company $300 million per year, but they pay nothing to the Aboriginal landowners. Instead, from the federal government coffers, Yolngu receive the lowest rate of royalties of any mine on Aboriginal land in Australia. Much of the country around Gove is now blighted. Toxic waste ponds occupy hunting grounds; alumina dust pollutes the air, and a mining town of 4000 occupies land within view of *Yolngu* communities. The processing plant expels chemical coolants into Melville Bay, and in 1990 it was discovered that unacceptably high levels of heavy metals, such as cadmium, had been dumped into the harbor, and Yolngu were warned not to eat shellfish.

The Yolngu have been constantly calling for an agreement with Alusuisse-Lonza. They desire sacred sites protection, fair monetary compensation, more business and employment opportunities, and access to information about the mine and its effects on the environment. Late in 1996, when no response was forthcoming, Yunupingu took the bold step of sending a delegation from northeast Arnhem Land to visit the mining company headquarters in Switzerland. Following intense discussions, there is now talk of the implementation of social and environmental impact studies, which are usually conducted prior to a development, to be funded by the company. For Yolngu, this is merely a prelude to native title compensation claims over the development site. Aborigines do not wish to see an end to the mining operation. In the spirit of reconciliation, they are prepared to work with miners, but only if they receive reasonable compensation. As discussed in the last chapter, Aborigines are prepared to pay their own way, but they desire just and honorable treatment.

A secondary form of protest against Alusuisse-Lonza has been underway since the early 1980s. Yunupingu and his brother Mandawuy are foundation members of the influential Yolngu rock band *Yothu Yindi*. For years this Yirrkala/Elcho Island group has been singing up-beat songs calling for respect for the rights of indigenous people and a better deal from developers. They have traveled the globe—to New York, London, Rome, and Paris—singing their protest songs, but their concerts are best remembered for the overwhelming, if fleeting, sense of reconciliation that is evoked when blacks and whites dance together on the world's stage.

REUNITING WITH THE MACASSANS

I discussed in Chapter 8 the travels of the Galiwin'ku Black Crusade throughout the desert regions of central Australia, bringing the "Good News" to Aborigines. Self-proclaimed banner-wavers for reconciliation, Yolngu Christians have traveled to Israel, Timor, Germany, and New Zealand and seek justice as an outcome of their call for unity in diversity. Warramiri Yolngu are pursuing a similar strategy: In 1988, a replica of a Macassan prau sailed to Arnhem Land and was met at Galiwin'ku by 500 Yolngu performing the ceremonies of Birrinydji. In 1996 Yolngu shared aspects of the Birrinydji Dreaming with Macassans as a means of reuniting with their old trading partners. On the beach at Galiwin'ku, in an event which could not even be contemplated in other parts of the country, Yolngu and Macassans embarked upon a dance exchange, a celebration of their joint histories, far removed from the notion of "Australia" and "Indonesia" as discrete entities. A further exchange took place in November 1997, but this time Yolngu took Birrinydji dances to Macassar. Personally endorsed by the governor of South Sulawesi and widely reported on Indonesian television and in the press, the ceremonial exchange was an enormous success.

Non-Aboriginal academics have written a great deal about the exotic historical episode of contact between Islamic fishermen and Aboriginal hunter-gatherers. For Macassans, the trip was a business venture. For Yolngu it was their first prolonged contact with non-Aborigines and the beginning of their involvement in the world economy. Arnhem Land, or Marege as Macassans called it, was the far-thest coast and one of the most lucrative of their sojourns at sea. All along northeast Arnhem Land beaches are traces of the presence of Asian traders: stone lines which once supported cooking pots; pottery shards and fragments of glass; and tamarind trees, which were place markers for the seasonal travelers. Despite many recorded episodes of violence and bloodshed, with the passing of time and the blurring of memories, the industry is remembered with great fondness by Aborigines.

Many Yolngu today view the heroic times of trade and travel to and from Macassar aboard sailing vessels as a golden era. Macassan seafarers were a hardy lot and it was the greatest of all adventures for a young Aborigine to embark upon the voyage to Sulawesi. Yolngu are now retracing by plane the voyage to Macassar, and some of them hope to make contact with long lost relatives.

Elcho Islanders believe that the renewal of a relationship with Macassans, a people whose presence in Arnhem Land predates the arrival of Europeans, will have consequences far beyond the antici-pated enjoyment of traveling once again to the exotic ports of south-east Asia. They view it as a step toward domestic recognition of Aboriginal sovereignty. In Burrumarra's mind, the two peoples were "one" in the law of Birrinydji and Walitha'walitha: The dance ex-change with Macassar created a model for the achievement of recon-ciliation, just as the erection of an Aboriginal Tent Embassy in Canberra in the 1970s strongly underscored the idea that Aborigines should be treated as the equal of the nations represented on Embassy Row. Yolngu are Australians, and proudly so, but their identity as Aborigines precedes and in some sense trumps that of the nation state. They assert dual citizenship, and claim rights and responsibili-ties to both Australia and to their Mala and homelands.

Burrumarra was also quick to point out that, with the exception of Christianity, no laws comparable to Birrinydji and Walitha'walitha united Aborigines and non-Aborigines in Australia. Thus, in detailing the way in which Aborigines and Macassans were aligned in the past, Burrumarra was commenting on the need for a similar set of laws to reconcile Australians. He saw the Flag Treaty proposal as being one step in this process. The dance exchange was another.

The ceremonial exchange was a show of solidarity with people who, while once rich and powerful, now enjoy a similarly low level of material wealth as Aborigines. Second, it demonstrated how Yolngu have kept the faith, and continue to perform the dances which they had once shared. Third, it opened the door for cross-cultural commu-nication and travel between Arnhem Land and Sulawesi.[29] Finally it

---

29. Ujung Pandang is a sister city to the Northern Territory capital, Darwin.

was a sign to non-Aboriginal authorities in Australia that the Yolngu are their own self-governing unit and should be treated as such.

The ability of Warramiri Aborigines to apply their cultural repertoire as a means of fostering relations with the Macassans provides a powerful commentary on the nature of relations between Aborigines and non-Aborigines in Australia today. Despite a similarly disastrous contact in the early years of colonization, they still ask: How can the various parties come together? What laws bind Yolngu and Balanda? An analysis of the way in which Yolngu are reaching out to the world through the qualities that make them unique is evidence that the international arena is an avenue for the pursuit of domestic reconciliation. Yolngu seek to affirm their rights in relation to non-Aborigines through face to face consultations with multinational corporations, by appeal to organizations such as the United Nations, and through symbolic gestures, like the international travels of the Black Crusade or the dance exchange with Macassans, on which the Warramiri place particular emphasis.

The knowledge that Yolngu are not alone in their struggle for justice is reassuring.[30] The coming together through law, whether indigenous, domestic, Biblical, or international, encompasses a recognition that different peoples have different opinions on those laws and on the past. Membership-and-remembership, as a policy, frees Yolngu from the confines of present restrictive governmental regulations and policies, and provides a space for deliberating future courses of action. Just as the Warramiri say they were united with whale hunters through the laws of the sea, with Macassans via Birrinydji and Walitha'walitha, with Christians through the blood of Jesus, and with other indigenous peoples through the shared experience of dispossesion, and now U.N. covenants; theoretically there can be partnerships between all peoples, but only if there is mutual recognition of each other's rights and beliefs.

---

30. The latest estimate is that there are 350 million indigenous people worldwide, or 5 percent of the earth's population, and the number is growing.

12

The Road Ahead

Despite the ground-breaking reconciliatory endeavours of clans such as the Warramiri, the road ahead for the divided nation is a troubled one. In this chapter I ask whether government can extinguish or severely curtail Aboriginal native title rights and still expect Aborigines and non-Aborigines to live together as a single nation; how Aborigines can pay their own way if they do not have security of tenure, economic self-reliance, and cultural integrity; and whether adoption, or membership-and-remembership, can become a policy that inspires the nation to establish cordial relations with its indigenous citizens.

PROGRESS AND REGRESS

In 1992, then Prime Minister Paul Keating set the tone for a reconciliation to come when he signaled the end of the "great Australian silence" on the past mistreatment of Aborigines. In a moving speech heralding the United Nations International Year for Indigenous Peoples, he stated that reconciliation was the "litmus test of Australian democracy." He said:

> We took the traditional lands and smashed the traditional
> way of life. We brought the diseases. The alcohol. We com-
> mitted the murders. We took the children from their moth-
> ers. We practiced discrimination and exclusion. It was our
> ignorance and our prejudice. And our failure to imagine
> these things being done to us. With some noble exceptions,
> we failed to make the most basic human response and enter
> into their hearts and minds. (Broome, 1996:70–71)

Reconciliation was to be a demonstration of Australia's maturation as a nation, its coming of age. The Australian people would reach an understanding of the Aboriginal experience and come to terms with their responsibility. This was in contrast to the past, when modernity was measured by the notion of progress, and the displacement of Aborigines was considered a necessary precondition.

When the Native Title Act was enacted in 1993, reconciliation appeared to be within the nation's grasp. Yet, only five years later in 1998, Prime Minister Howard's "compromise" deal amending this legislation seemed certain to curtail the momentum for reform. According to Pat Dodson, former chair of the Council for Aboriginal Reconciliation, the 1998 revisions to the act are "Catch 22"—like the poisoning of the waterholes of long ago. The Mabo High Court decision affirmed that Aborigines do not need to have "whitefella" paper in order to prove their native title. It exists in common law. Yet revisions to the Act require that in order to enjoy such rights, native title must be proven before a "whitefella" court—and access to that court is becoming more and more complicated. Also, native title rights are only deemed to exist if Aborigines had physical access to their land not more than two generations ago, which, as Aboriginal activist Noel Pearson says, is tantamount to rewarding pastoralists for past policies of eviction.

In his research into reconciliation, anthropologist Ron Brunton discovered that 54 percent of Australia's indigenous population lived in households that contained one or more nonindigenous persons. This, he said, was evidence that the gulf between Aborigines and other Australians is not as great as many would have us believe (*Courier-Mail,* June 2, 1998). In fact, he sees a fundamental contradiction at the heart of the reconciliation debate. On the one hand there are Aborigines and non-Aborigines who genuinely accept the vision of the Council for Aboriginal Reconciliation. On the other, some Australians busily promote the guilt industry and try to use reconciliation as a political lever. The present Australian prime minister has expressed the belief that reconciliation and, in particular, our national Sorry Day on May 26, dedicated to those from the "Stolen Generation" still trying to find their way home, is being driven by a left-wing agenda (*Courier-Mail* June 1, 1998). If this contradiction is to be resolved, Brunton says, reconciliation must be set apart from local and national disputes. Yet Brunton has not speculated on what adoption or membership-and-remembership means to traditionally-minded Aborigines. Historian Henry Reynolds argues that Australia can have reconciliation or it can embrace the federal government's Native Title Act amendments. It cannot have both. The High Court opened the door to reconciliation and beckoned Australia toward partnership, sharing, and negotiation (*Courier-Mail,* June 2, 1998). Yet now, rather than having a right to negotiate over land to which they have a native title interest, Aborigines may only request heritage protection for significant cultural sites, should they be in danger of disturbance during mining operations. Reynolds points out that the curtailment of native title contravenes Australia's international obligations under two of the world's key human rights documents, the International Covenant on Civil and Political Rights and the Convention on the Elimination of All Forms of Racial Discrimination.

Amendments to the Native Title Act have divided the nation. One segment of the populace, in particular members and supporters of Pauline Hanson's popular One Nation Party, believes the prime minister's concessions in this compromise plan were far too generous. ATSIC spokesperson Geoff Clarke and Aboriginal supporters, on the other hand, viewed the amendments as a return to pre-Mabo days and even *terra nullius*. Like the Yolngu, Clarke believes that reconciliation should involve an Australia-wide agreement between government and each and every clan. For those whose native title rights have not been recognized by Balanda law, this is an important first step. Burrumarra envisaged this in his Flag Treaty proposal, and looked to indigenous groups throughout Australia to make a public statement on their commitment to reconciliation. Aborigines and Torres Strait Islanders would combine in a single design sacred symbols from their own "country" with those representing the dominant culture. In other words, reconciliation and rights to land and sea go hand in hand.

The Council for Aboriginal Reconciliation had anticipated the prime minister's handling of the situation. In 1995 and 1996, it unsuccessfully attempted to establish a constructive dialogue between government, farmers, miners, and Aborigines on Aboriginal property rights. The federal government stood by its equality before the law position that Aborigines are just one group in the society with no more nor less rights than other groups. Other Australians did not have a right to negotiate over what happens on their land, so why should Aborigines? In 1997, South African President Nelson Mandela offered to act as a mediator between Aborigines and the federal government with respect to the future of Aboriginal land rights, but when Prime Minister Howard refused to budge on any of his ten points, negotiations fell through. In response, Aborigines formed the National Indigenous Working Group on Native Title and, in a pamphlet entitled "Negotiation and Certainty," clearly laid out their position. First and foremost Aborigines must have a right to negotiate regarding developments on land for which they have a native title interest. Then there must be

• no extinguishment of title without the informed consent of the native title holders

• no precluding towns or waterways from native title claims

• no sunset clause on native title claims

But on July 1, 1998, the government indicated that it had the numbers in the Senate to push through a package of amendments that satisfied the miners, pastoralists, and conservative state governments. Only the controversial One Nation Party and Aborigines and Torres Strait Islanders were disgruntled, the former believing, for instance, that Australia's indigenous people already enjoyed too much power and influence.

In this very unstable atmosphere, a huge groundswell of non-Aboriginal support for native title has emerged among Australia's rank and file in the form of a People's Movement for Reconciliation and Justice. The number of grassroots organizations promoting reconciliation has increased from 10 to 229. Phil Glendenning, national coordinator of Australians for Native Title and Reconciliation (ANTAR), says that this rallying of public support for a cause has been unmatched since the Vietnam War. The "Sea of Hands" sculptures are an expression of this movement.[31]

In 1998, Australians appeared ready to endorse a new constitutional preamble that recognized the unique position of the nation's indigenous inhabitants as the former owners of the land. But reconciliation is more than words. If one examines the arguments on reconciliation discussed in Chapters 2 and 3, it appears that mutual understanding will occur between indigenous and nonindigenous Australians only when there is a resolution of arguments concerning economics, human rights, and identity. There must be the following

Human Rights Reconciliation

- recognition that Aborigines did not cede sovereignty to the British in 1788
- a restructuring of the administration of Aboriginal affairs to facilitate self-determination
- a solution for unemployment, alcohol-related and violence problems that beset the Aboriginal community

Economic Reconciliation

- the efficient management of tax dollars earmarked for Aboriginal affairs
- an end to the making of fraudulent claims by Aborigines in order to forestall a development or get a larger stake in the profits
- a realization that indigenous people have a right to basic community services, no more nor less than anyone else

Identity Reconciliation

- a willingness by non-Aborigines to learn from Aborigines and Torres Strait Islanders
- an acceptance by both Aborigines and non-Aborigines that their histories are intertwined

---

31. When the amendments to the Native Title Act were enacted, the "Sea of Hands" sculpture was rearranged to spell out the word *shame*.

In September 1998, Australia was a long way from achieving these prerequisites. The Indigenous Working Group on Native Title has warned of massive compensation bills if and when Aboriginal native title rights are extinguished as a consequence of amendments to the act; of High Court challenges to the 1998 amendments; as well as possible trade sanctions. They, at least, wish to keep the reconciliation process on track.

RECONCILIATION IN ARNHEM LAND

Residents of Galiwin'ku live outside the mainstream of Australian politics and in some sense they represent a special case. They were never removed from their land as was the case in other parts of the nation. Under provisions of the Aboriginal Land Rights Act they also have the power of veto over development, a right that Aborigines in other Australian states and territories do not enjoy. One might presume that Elcho Islanders should have fewer complaints than other Aborigines, but this is not the case. They are not exempt, for example, from the problems endemic to Australia's indigenous populations. Three clans have become extinct in the past forty years, and more than forty over the past 200 years according to one estimate. For the Warramiri, school attendance and performance is unacceptably low, and petrol sniffing and kava consumption is rife. The incidence of disease stemming from unsanitary and overcrowded living conditions is on the increase, and money is always in short supply. Advocates of the genocide view on reconciliation use these statistics as evidence of the need for a better deal for Aborigines.

Most businesses at Galiwin'ku, like the store and "take-away" are owned by non-Aborigines. The few profitable enterprises open to Aborigines are in areas of dubious legality, such as the importation of kava from Tonga or Fiji, the unauthorized hiring and sales of videos, or high-risk "grog" running. In the equality before the law idea on reconciliation, Aborigines are accused of expecting a dramatic turnaround in their fortunes without working for it. What is required is an opportunity for Aborigines to manage their own viable enterprises; for this to happen business leaders must turn their eyes from the short-term financial balance sheet and, as Barrie Thomas of "The Body Shop" says, look to the social balance sheet. However, there is little evidence of such an attitude at Galiwin'ku.

For Elcho Islanders reconciliation is not just saying sorry, or lending a helping hand to Aborigines in order to get a business started, or even the provision of funding to improve Aboriginal living conditions. It has a religious as well as a political dimension. Just as Aborigines have adopted non-Aborigines at both the group and individual level, non-Aborigines must also adopt Aborigines and adhere to Aboriginal law. Self-determination for Yolngu, the object of the adoption process, would entail the acknowledgement of land and sea rights and participation and partnerships in the management and utilization of resources. One substantial barrier to the achievement of these goals is non-Aboriginal law itself: acts of Parliament that restrict Aboriginal ownership of country to the low watermark; that limit the involvement of indigenous people in seas management; and that promote mining through a process locally referred to as "humbug."

There is overwhelming agreement from both Aborigines and non-Aborigines that respect and face-to-face negotiations are essential ingredients for reconciliation. For advocates of the pay-your-own-way school of thought, when Aborigines sit down and negotiate a fair deal for opening their land to development, then Aborigines will begin to enjoy better housing, schools, community centers, gardens and the like. But Yolngu arguing for justice-before-reconciliation respond by saying, "Why do we have to have mining in order to enjoy our basic human rights?" Representatives of industry, stressing equality-before-the-law, have said that Aborigines will need viable industries in order to survive, and they can lend a hand; but as Aboriginal academic Marcia Langton points out, Aborigines are suspected of desiring rights that no one else enjoys. Alternatively, non-Aboriginal advocates of the no-indigenous-viewpoint school of thought will assert that Aborigines have lost all contact with the land and do not follow the traditions of old, so it is unreasonable of them to expect compensation if, for example, a sacred site is disturbed during a big budget project bringing vital export dollars into the national coffers.

The Future of Reconciliation

For Yolngu at Galiwin'ku, the Dreaming is a positive influence in the debate for a rapprochement between Aborigines and non-Aborigines. It provides a way of seeing through the seemingly mutually exclusive preconditions for reconciliation, for at its very core is the ideology of adoption or membership-and-remembership. Macassans were adopted en masse in the trepang era by the Yirritja moiety, providing Yolngu with a mandate for the pursuit of equity with non-Aborigines. In the mission period, non-Aborigines were adopted on an individual basis, on their merits as potential brokers for a better deal for Galiwin'ku residents. The non-Aboriginal assimilation policy was also an attempt at adoption, but it was unsatisfactory according to Aborigines, for it failed to take into account the specificities of their culture. This same criticism was leveled at the techniques employed by governments for the implementation of the policy of self-determination. In the past ten years, Yolngu have endeavored to clarify to non-

Aborigines what self-determination and, consequently, reconciliation mean in their agitation for sea rights, proper dealings with development companies, and in finding a voice in the international arena. Warramiri support for reconciliation is therefore to be viewed not as product of non-Aboriginal policies or programs, but rather in spite of them. Through a process of membership-and-remembership, Dreaming beliefs provide the means for Warramiri Yolngu to build ties with select individuals, who become active and supportive members of the moiety, clan, and family; with faith communities, who spread the word of unity through shared belief in Christianity; and with Fourth World peoples, who plead the case of self-determination and land rights at forums such as the United Nations.

Burrumarra saw the role of the Dreaming in reconciliation in a more traditional sense than do Warramiri of the present generation. In the 1950s, he believed that if Yolngu had access to training and resources in the mission, they could enter the modern world on their own terms. He and Badangga would change the Dreaming to allow a place for Christianity, for this was to be their point of entry into the non-Aboriginal world. In the last year of his life, Burrumarra said that only when reconciliation between Aborigines and non-Aborigines was achieved, will Birrinydji have fulfilled his promise. Reconciliation, from this perspective, is an outcome of ritual practice associated with the Dreaming, for it promises a return to the status quo envisaged by followers of Aboriginal law. At some point in the far distant past, white and black were "members" of one religious community, and Yolngu learnt from non-Aborigines, but both benefitted materially from having access to Aboriginal land.

Can membership-and-remembership become a policy that inspires the non-Aboriginal community? In the town of Galiwin'ku, levels of membership include the church, the school, the moiety, clan, family, and peer group. When Yolngu visit Darwin on diplomatic missions, it is as envoys for the Yolngu as a whole, of both moieties. Yet when Aboriginal member of Parliament Wes Lanhupuy returned home to Elcho Island after house sittings, he would be treated not as a visiting dignitary, but as one of the youngest sons of Badangga and therefore answerable to his brothers, and people such as Burrumarra, whom he called father. He would join in the storytelling around the fire at night and share stories of city life with his friends and family. At any one time, numerous levels of membership come into play, and it is important to recognize concomitant responsibilities. Wes was a politician representing black and white Australians, a member of the Labor Party, but also a Yolngu and a member of a clan and family. A certain amount of juggling is required to follow party lines in a parliamentary debate on legislation that may promote or alternatively adversely affect some Aborigines, and still represent one's Aboriginal constituents, friends, and associates. But this is the struggle confronting those intent on making reconciliation a living reality in the lives of all Australians.

Within the non-Aboriginal community, membership-and-remembership can be acknowledged in a number of ways. Non-Aboriginal Australians have tasted the spirituality of the land, Djiniyini Gondarra says, even if they are not aware of it. They have also benefited materially from either extracting resources from the land or sea or by growing produce from soil enriched by the blood of the ancestors. At this level, non-Aborigines are "members" of a nation for which Aborigines are custodians. Therefore they "come under" Aborigines. But on the other hand, Aborigines require the establishment of industries on their homelands and training in order to take advantage of the opportunities being provided by non-Aborigines. "We can share the continent together," Burrumarra said, as he contemplated the sacred center of a new community with its foundation in the Dreaming.

Despite the ground-breaking efforts of Yolngu, the exalted thoughts and actions of some advocates of reconciliation and the encouraging words of overseas experts, the future of Aboriginal reconciliation is in the hands of politicians and at the mercy of the political process. Only a minority of Australian parliamentarians have any idea of what Aborigines think, and still fewer care. The pursuit of political power and accommodating the agenda of the multinational corporate sector is of uppermost concern. Under the present federal regime, reconciliation appears to be a lost cause. Yolngu history over the past forty years provides insight into what is required for reconciliation to succeed. Reconciliation must entail the recognition of their land and sea rights and also self-determination for Aborigines and Torres Strait Islanders. Yet few existing federal or state laws promote reconciliation, and where they do, they are under threat. The future holds three possibilities: (1) the likelihood of improved relations between Aborigines and non-Aborigines if the Labor Party attains power; (2) the slow erosion of Aboriginal rights and the reconciliation process if a conservative liberal-national government retains power; or (3) the cessation of the reconciliation process and the extinguishment of Aboriginal native title throughout Australia if Pauline Hanson's One Nation Party ever achieves the balance of power in the federal Parliament. For Elcho Islanders, Aboriginal reconciliation has its foundation in the Dreaming, but for politicians and many non-Aborigines it is but a pipe dream—pretty-sounding words with little substance.

Glossary

Badu   In Warramiri mythology it is the land of the dead to the northeast of Arnhem Land.

Balanda   Non-Aboriginal, a European and/or Macassan.

Bandirra   Flag.

Bayini   The wife of Birrinydji, an ancestor for Warramiri peoples, and a term given for the second wave of visitors to Arnhem Land.

Birrinydji   "Man of iron," or "King of the Murrnginy"; a creation figure associated with the Yirritja moiety.

Bukulatjpi   A historical Warramiri leader credited with "discovering" Birrinydji.

Bunggawa   Aboriginal leader and/or Macassan captain.

Bunggul   An Aboriginal dance or ceremony.

Dholtji   Warramiri homeland.

Dhuwa   The northeast Arnhem Land social and cultural world is divided into halves or moieties. One is Dhuwa and the other Yirritja.

Djang'kawu   Major creation and ancestral figure in Dhuwa mythology.

Garma   Public or "outside" knowledge or *Rom*.

Gunapipi   Sacred Dhuwa moiety Aboriginal ceremony associated with the rainbow serpent.

Lany'tjun   Major creation and ancestral figure in Yirritja mythology.

Macassan   A composite term for seafarers and trepangers, also known as Bugis, Macassarese, and Sama-Bajau (sea gypsies).

Macassar (Makassar)   Ujung Pandang, South Sulawesi.

Madayin   Object or idea of religious or ceremonial significance.

Mala   Clan group.

Manikay   Song.

Murrnginy (Murngin)   A word referring to the "pre-Macassan" iron age of Birrinydji, though once used by Warner (1937) to refer to a collection of Dhuwa and Yirritja clan groups. It now refers to the

Warramiri, Gumatj, Dhalwangu, Wangurri, and Gupapuyngu-Birrkili Mala, who share Birrinydji information.

Ngaarra   Sacred ceremony for a Mala.

Rangga   Sacred objects.

Rom   Yolngu law.

Walitha'walitha   Allah, a creation figure in Warramiri mythology; associated with Birrinydji and Wurramu.

Wangarr   Creational period.

Wurramu   Spirit of the dead in Yirritja mythology.

Yirritja   A moiety, see Dhuwa.

Yolngu   An Aboriginal from northeast Arnhem Land.

Yolngu Matha   Aboriginal languages of northeast Arnhem Land.

References

Allen, D.
1994. Salt-Water Dreaming. In P. Jull et al. (eds.), *Surviving Columbus. Indigenous Peoples, Political Reform and Environmental Management in North Australia*. North Australia Research Unit, Darwin.

ARDS (Aboriginal Resource and Development Services Inc.).
1994. Cross-Cultural Awareness Education for Aboriginal People. A consultancy for the Office of Aboriginal Development, Darwin.

Barnier, C. (ed.).
1978. *Notable Australians: The Pictorial Who's Who*. Prestige Publishing, Sydney.

Berndt, R. M.
1962. *An Adjustment Movement in Arnhem Land*. Cahiers de L'Homme, Mouton, Paris and The Hague.

Berndt, R. M. & Berndt, C. H.
1954. *Arnhem Land. Its History and Its People*. F. W. Cheshire, Melbourne.

Borsboom, A. P.
1992. Millenarianism, Australian Aborigines and the European Myth of Primitives. *Canberra Anthropology* 15(2):11–26.

Bos, R.
1988. The Dreaming and Social Change in Arnhem Land. In T. Swain and D. Rose (eds.), *Aboriginal Australians and Christian Missions: Ethnographic and Historical Studies (Special Studies in Religion No. 6)*, 442–437. Australian Association for the Study of Religions, Bedford Park.

Bravo, K. E.
Balancing Indigenous Rights to Land and the Demands of Economic Development: Lessons from the United States and Australia. Columbia Journal of Law and Social Problems. 30(4):529–586.

Broome, R.
1996. Historians, Aborigines and Australia: Writing the National Past. In B. Attwood (ed.), *In the Age of Mabo. History, Aborigines and Australia*, 54–72. Allen & Unwin, Sydney.

Buber, M.
1949. *Paths in Utopia*. Beacon Press, Boston.

Burrumarra D. n.d. Dhawal'yuwa Yuwalku.
The Search for Truth. Lodged in AIATSIS Library, Canberra.

Burridge, K.
1971. *New Heaven New Earth. A Study of Millenarian Activities.* Basil Blackwell, Oxford.

Cawte, J.
1993. *The Universe of the Warramirri. Art, Medicine and Religion in Arnhem Land.* University of New South Wales Press, Sydney.

Collmann, J.
1988. Fringe-Dwellers and Welfare. The Aboriginal Response to Bureaucracy. University of Queensland Press, St Lucia.

Commonwealth of Australia.
1976. *Aboriginal Land Rights (Northern Territory) Act.* Australian Government Publishers, Canberra.

Coombs, H. C.
1994. *Aboriginal Autonomy. Issues and Strategies.* Cambridge University Press, Melbourne.

Council for Aboriginal Reconciliation.
1997. *The Path to Reconciliation: Issues for a People's Movement.* Australian Government Publishing, Canberra.

Cowlishaw, G.
1998. Erasing Culture and Race: Practicing "Self-Determination." *Oceania* 68(3):148–169.

Flinders, M.
1814. *A Voyage to Terra Australis.* G. and W. Nichol, London.

Freire, P.
1973. *Education for Critical Consciousness.* Seabury Press, New York.

Garrawurra, J. R.
1982. Untitled article in *Crucible* (Uniting Church in Australia, Northern Synod), May.

Ginydjirrang Mala.
1994. *Manbuynga ga Rulyapa. A Call for an Indigenous Marine Strategy for the Arafura Sea.* Ocean Rescue 2000.

Gondarra, D.
1988. *Father You Gave Us the Dreaming.* Uniting Church of Australia, Darwin.

Jarrat, P.
1992. Australia's Forgotten Islands. The English Company's Group. *The Bulletin,* January 28–February 4, 126–133.

Keen, I.
1994. *Knowledge and Secrecy in an Aboriginal Religion. Yolngu of North-East Arnhem Land.* Oxford Studies in Social and Cultural Anthropology. Clarendon Press, Oxford.

Kolig, E.
1981. *The Silent Revolution. The Effects of Modernization on Australian Aboriginal Religion.* Institute for the Study of Human Issues, Philadelphia.

Kolig, E.
1989. *Dreamtime Politics: Religion, World View, and Utopian Thought in Australian Aboriginal Society.* Deitrich Rehmer Verlag, Berlin.

Lattas
1997.   Aborigines and Contemporary Australian Nationalism: Primordiality
         and the Cultural Politics of Otherness. In G. Cowlishaw (ed.), *Race Mat-
         ters*, pp. 223–255. University of Queensland Press, St Lucia.
Linnekin, J.
1992.   On the Theory and Politics of Cultural Construction in the Pacific. *Oce-
         ania* 62(4):249–263.
Macknight, C. C.
1976.   *The Voyage to Marege. Macassan Trepangers in Northern Australia.*Mel-
         bourne University Press, Melbourne.
Maddock, K.
1972.   *The Australian Aborigines. A Portrait of Their Society.* Penguin, Melbourne.
Marika-Mununggiritj, R.
1991.   How Can Balanda (White Australians) Learn About the Aboriginal
         World? *Ngoonjook. Batchelor Journal of Aboriginal Education 5* (July):17–25.
McIntosh, I.
1992.   The Bricoleur at Work: Warang (Dingo) Mythology in the Yirritja
         Moiety of North-East Arnhem Land. Master of Letters thesis, University
         of New England, Armidale.
McIntosh, I. S.
1994.   *The Whale and the Cross. Conversations with David Burrumarra, M.B.E.* His-
         torical Society of the Northern Territory, Darwin.
McIntosh, I. S.
1996.   Can We Be Equal in Your Eyes? A Perspective on Reconciliation from
         North-East Arnhem Land. Unpublished PhD thesis, Northern Territory
         University.
Morgan, M.
1994.   *Mutant Message Down Under.* HarperCollins, New York.
Morphy, H.
1983.   "Now You Understand." An Analysis of the Way Yolngu Have Used
         Sacred Knowledge to Retain Their Identity. In N. Peterson and M. Lang-
         ton (eds.), *Aborigines, Land and Land Rights,* 110–133. Australian Institute
         of Aboriginal Studies Press, Canberra.
Morphy, H.
1990.   Myth, Totemism and the Creation of Clans. *Oceania* 60(4):312–328.
O'Faircheallaigh, C.
1995.   Mineral Development Agreements Negotiated by Aboriginal Commu-
         nities in the 1990s. CAEPR Discussion Paper No. 85. Australian Nation-
         al University, Canberra.
Palmer, K. and Brady, M.
1983.   *Aboriginal Rights to Land in the Wessel Archipelago. The Politics of Land
         Tenure among the Yolngu of North-East Arnhem Land.* Northern Land
         Council, Darwin.
Read, P. and Read, J.
1991.   *Long Time, Olden Time. Aboriginal Accounts of Northern Territory History.*
         Institute for Aboriginal Development Publications, Alice Springs.
Reynolds, H.
1998.   *This Whispering in Our Hearts.* Allen and Unwin, Sydney.

Rudder, J.
  1993.   Yolngu Cosmology. An Unchanging Cosmos Incorporating a Rapidly
           Changing World? Unpublished PhD Thesis, Australian National Uni-
           versity, Canberra.

Sahlins, M.
  1981.   *Historical Metaphors and Mythical Realities: Structure in the Early History of
           the Sandwich Islands Kingdoms.* Association for the Study of Anthropology
           in Oceania, Special Publication No. 1, University of Michigan, Ann
           Arbor.

Sahlins, M.
  1985.   *Islands of History.* University of Chicago Press, Chicago.

Shepherdson, E.
  1981.   *Half a Century in Arnhem Land.* E & H Shepherdson, One Tree Hill,
           South Australia.

Sorrenson, K.
  1991.   Treaties in British Colonial Policy: Precedents for Waitangi. In W. Ren-
           wick (ed.). *Sovereignty & Indigenous Rights. The Treaty of Waitangi in Inter-
           national Contexts,* pp. 15–29, Victoria University Press, Wellington.

Stanner, W. E. H.
  1958.   The Dreaming. In W. A. Lessa and E. Z. Vogt (eds.), *Reader in Compara-
           tive Religion: An Anthropological Approach.* Row Peterson, Evanston.

Supreme Court of Northern Territory.
  1971.   *Milirrpum and Others versus Nabalco and the Commonwealth of Australia,*
           Darwin.

Traube, E. G.
  1986.   *Cosmology and Social Life: Ritual Exchange Among the Mambai of East
           Timor.* University of Chicago Press, Chicago.

Warner, W. L.
  1958/69. *A Black Civilization. A Social Study of an Australian Tribe.* Harper & Roe,
           Chicago.

Williams, N. M.
  1986.   *The Yolngu and Their Land: A System of Land Tenure and the Fight for Its
           Recognition.* A.I.A.T.S.I.S., Canberra.

Woodward, Justice.
  1974.   Aboriginal Land Rights Commission, Second Report.

Yumbulul, T., and Djinyini, K.
  1996.   My Island Home—A Marine Protection Strategy for Manbuynga ga
           Rulyapa. In *Land Rights Past, Present and Future.* Conference Proceed-
           ings, pp. 107–109. Northern and Central Land Councils, Darwin and
           Alice Springs.

Index